Elstree
THE BRITISH HOLLYWOOD

Thorn-EMI Elstree Studios, Borehamwood, Hertfordshire, 1982

Patricia Warren

Foreword by Dame Anna Neagle

ELM TREE BOOKS · LONDON

*This book is dedicated to
everyone who has ever
participated in the making of
Elstree: The British Hollywood,
through the decades to the
present day – with affection and
gratitude.*

First published in Great Britain 1983
by Elm Tree Books/Hamish Hamilton Ltd
Garden House 57–59 Long Acre London WC2E 9JZ

Copyright © 1983 by Patricia Warren

Book design by Norman Reynolds
Picture research by Patricia Warren

The endpapers show Adrienne Ames in scenes
from *Abdul the Damned*

British Library Cataloguing in Publication Data

Warren, Patricia
    Elstree.
    1. Moving-picture industries—Elstree (Hertfordshire)
    —History
    I. Title
    384′.8′09425895   PN1993.5.G/
    ISBN 0-241-10955-8

Printed in Great Britain by
BAS Printers Ltd, Over Wallop, Hampshire

Contents

Foreword
by Dame Anna Neagle

I have so many happy memories of Elstree that I am only too delighted to contribute, albeit in a small way, to a book which affectionately and with pride sets out to tell its story without rancour or pointless criticism.

Elstree: The British Hollywood is a well chosen title, for Elstree is unique in that it is the only British film *colony* to date. That distinction attracted not only the cream of our own industry, but talents from the United States and the Continent as well.

My late husband, Herbert Wilcox, came to Elstree towards the end of the 1920s, formed his own Company and Studios, British and Dominions, becoming a neighbour of John Maxwell's British International Picture complex next door.

From the making of *Goodnight Vienna* in 1932 Elstree was to become not only my second home, but also a very important part of my life. It was a life filled with actors, directors, writers and film technicians, all engaged in establishing this creative British film centre. One can only marvel at the vision and courage it required to compete against the overwhelming competition of the American films which provided the bulk of entertainment for the many hundreds of cinemas throughout Great Britain.

Our sense of history and humour has stood us in good stead throughout the centuries and is reflected in many films produced at Elstree.

It is perhaps true to say that other nations have represented life in more realistic, even more passionate ways but, looking back, the wide spectrum produced at the Elstree Studios in those early days is quite remarkable. Examples which immediately spring to mind are pre-war gems such as *Blackmail, Blossom Time, Lord Camber's Ladies, Dandy Dick*, filmed at B.I.P.; and at British and Dominions, the Aldwych Farces *Rookery Nook* and *Thark*, Jack Buchanan musicals, *Carnival*, and *Nell Gwyn*, which had the dubious honour of being banned in the United States! It was here too, that Alexander Korda made the picture which made perhaps a greater impact throughout the world than any previous British film, *Henry VIII*.

Elstree, together with Gainsborough, Gaumont British and other studios, was gradually gaining strength – by 1936, with the opening of Korda's Denham Studios and Rank's Studios at Pinewood, the British film industry was becoming a force to be reckoned with.

Our national diffidence has far too often prevented us from extolling our own virtues and expertise at home and abroad – we are, as a nation, always so ready to criticise ourselves. I am glad, therefore, to have been invited to add my thoughts to a book which tells the story of one of our major studios and its contribution to an industry which, in spite of many difficulties still manages to produce films of international stature and profitability.

Even while Britain was engaged in war Elstree continued to hold a mirror to our way of life. Whilst some studios were requisitioned to make war equipment, others managed to keep up a steady stream of entertainment so essential in those dark and anxious days, a help in keeping up morale.

And then there were stories to be told of the heroism and astonishing unselfishness, emotions that manifest themselves most strongly in times of stress. Every aspect of war was filmed in a way which we know best – realism without sensationalism; heroism without sentimentality.

I will never forget my own feelings during the filming of *Odette*, nor the sense of pride and 'belonging' remembering such films as A.B.P.C.'s *The Hasty Heart* and *The Dambusters* and Noel Coward's *In Which We Serve*.

The ending of hostilities was a time when the British Hollywood really began to live up to its name. It was a time when a flood of cinematic luminaries from across the Atlantic began, each bringing their own individual magic to join with our own artists, once again fully committed to the world of entertainment.

Everyone connected with the old B.I.P., A.B.P.C. Studios and later EMI Studios has maintained an organisation which contributed enormously towards the rapid development of a British film industry, endeavouring to ensure that, come what may, Elstree will remain the heart of the British film production.

Elstree has given birth to many ideas and hundreds of films. B.I.P.'s descendants have much to give the movie world, be it their creativity or their technical expertise which is second to none.

In wishing this book success it is my fervent hope that Elstree will for many generations to come remain 'That Rock on which the British Film Industry is based'.

Anna Neagle

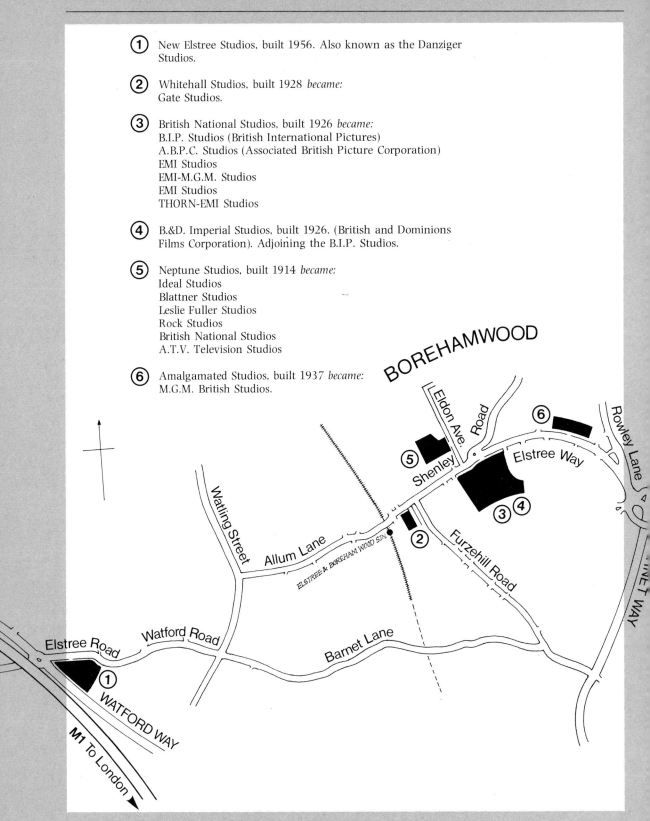

1. New Elstree Studios, built 1956. Also known as the Danziger Studios.

2. Whitehall Studios, built 1928 *became:*
   Gate Studios.

3. British National Studios, built 1926 *became:*
   B.I.P. Studios (British International Pictures)
   A.B.P.C. Studios (Associated British Picture Corporation)
   EMI Studios
   EMI-M.G.M. Studios
   EMI Studios
   THORN-EMI Studios

4. B.&D. Imperial Studios, built 1926. (British and Dominions Films Corporation). Adjoining the B.I.P. Studios.

5. Neptune Studios, built 1914 *became:*
   Ideal Studios
   Blattner Studios
   Leslie Fuller Studios
   Rock Studios
   British National Studios
   A.T.V. Television Studios

6. Amalgamated Studios, built 1937 *became:*
   M.G.M. British Studios.

BOREHAMWOOD

Eldon Ave.

Shenley

Road

Rowley Lane

Elstree Way

Watling Street

Allum Lane

ELSTREE & BOREHAM WOOD STN.

Furzehill Road

Elstree Road

Watford Road

Barnet Lane

WATFORD WAY

M1 To London

Introduction

I did not set out to write a book. My objective was to research a television programme on the subject of Elstree. Bookshops and libraries boasted books on Pinewood studios, Ealing studios, cinema histories, British cinema and so on, but there was no latter-day volume on the Elstree Studios, major contributors to our British cinema, film history and industry.

As my television research developed, so did *Elstree: The British Hollywood* in my mind. I hoped that it would go away – it did not. Armed with my research skeleton I confronted Andrew Mitchell, the Managing Director of Thorn-EMI Elstree Studios. Here was someone who would lay the ghost once and for all and point me in the direction of at least one new tome and a minimum of ten dusty old ones. This was not to be the case. He agreed with alacrity that an up-to-date book on Elstree Studios, from 1914 to the present day, was overdue and necessary, not only as a record for the industry, film students and film 'buffs', but also as an entertaining read. He took a keen and critical look at my research skeleton – and opened his doors. They proved to be very exclusive.

They were doors to film vaults, libraries, records and most important of all, people. Robert Clark, Robert Lennard, Erik Maxwell, Jack Middleton, Dame Anna Neagle, John Wilcox and many more. It is these famous and dedicated people, who have worked at Elstree from the early twenties to the present day, who have assisted my research so generously. Each in turn opened up new avenues of thought and research, making a point of introducing me to stars and personalities, who have worked and are working at Elstree. Continuity girls, makeup artists, secretaries, studio managers, producers and directors.

Two main points arose from these interviews and research:

1. That when one talks of Elstree, it is not one building or company such as Pinewood, Ealing or Denham, but the glamour and excitement of a British Hollywood, with its main B.I.P. studio complex (now Thorn-EMI Elstree) and many satellite companies and studios.

2. A sense of incredulous surprise that no recent book on Elstree had been published. The prestigious B.F.I. library took no joy in confirming that the last publication on Elstree Studios currently on their shelves was *The Elstree Story*, a booklet by Leslie Banks and Friends, written in 1947/1948.

It did not take me over-long to discover why this was the case. The very fact that one was dealing with a film township and community, as opposed to a single studio history, produced a horrendous amount of cross-referenced, contradictory material. For example, for technical or 'overflow' reasons, a number of films were started at one Elstree studio and finished at another. In some cases B.I.P.'s Elstree films would be partly completed at their Welwyn studios and vice-versa. Hundreds of independent producers over the decades changed from one Elstree studio to another – and so on.

The research and interviews dictated the type of book that should be written: an affectionate chronicle of life before and behind the cameras at Elstree from 1914 to the present day. A volume that I hope film buffs and the public will enjoy for its entertainment value and nostalgic pleasure along with its two hundred photographs and stills, in many cases donated by the participants.

Elstree: The British Hollywood would have been an impossible task without the people, skill and determination that went to make its history and the incredibly patient help and kindness that has manifested itself throughout the entire project.

Acknowledgements

THIS book would not have been possible without the unstinting help, support and enthusiasm that was received from literally everyone I approached for interviews, research and information.

But my special thanks, in the first instance, must go to Andrew Mitchell, Managing Director of Thorn-EMI Elstree Studios; Jack Middleton, Head of Library Services, Thorn-EMI Elstree Studios; and many of the studios' personnel who have contributed so wonderfully to the project, including Wendy Smith and the studios' Stills Department.

I am extremely grateful to Michelle Snapes and the stills and library service of the British Film Institute, Bermans and Nathans, I.T.C. Entertainments, Thames Television and private contributors for those stills that were not directly supplied from the impressive Thorn-EMI Elstree Studios stills library. Every effort has been made to trace the copyright holders of the photographs and quoted material. Should there be any omissions in this respect, we apologise and shall be pleased to make the appropriate acknowledgement in future editions.

My special thanks also go to Gerry Blattner, Lord Brabourne, Robert Clark, Michael Denison, Dulcie Gray, Marcel Hellman, Bryan Langley, Robert Lennard, Erik Maxwell, Kenneth Maidment, Dame Anna Neagle, Ian Scott, Richard Todd, John and Elizabeth Wilcox and Freddie Young, for their particular participation in the research interviews and to everyone who gave their time, advice and information.

My appreciation and gratitude go to Roger Houghton, Editorial Director of Elm Tree Books and my editor Caroline Taggart, who with enthusiastic no nonsense guidance, took the new girl in hand and licked her into some sort of shape, and finally, but by no means least, to my husband Andrew Warren, for much of the additional research and his marvellous support throughout the entire project.

I would like to thank the following for their kind assistance in the provision of stills for this book.

The Thorn-EMI Stills Library, Bermans and Nathans, Gerry Blattner, British Film Institute Stills Library, Daily Express, Daily Mirror, Hertfordshire Local Studies Collection, Hertfordshire Library Service, I.T.C. Entertainment – an A.C.C. Company, Bryan Langley, Erik Maxwell, Dame Anna Neagle, Python (Monty) Pictures Ltd, The Rank Organisation/M.A.M. (Film Productions) Ltd. and Apollo Leisure Group, Henry John Smith, Thames Television, Woodcote Productions Ltd/Warner Brothers.

Cartoons by courtesy of PUNCH.

Chapter 1

Elstree:
'Tall Oaks From Little Acorns Grow'

"HOLD THAT, JOHN!"

UNCLE SAM: "HELLO, BRITISHER, GOING IN FOR FILM-MAKING? DON'T FORGET OUR OLD SONG, 'WE'VE GOT THE SUN, WE'VE GOT THE STARS, AN' WE'VE GOT THE MONEY TOO.'"

JOHN BULL (registering dogged determination): "NO MATTER, I'M GOING TO HAVE A TRY."

PLEASE read the titles to yourself. Loud reading annoys your neighbours.

By the time Percy Nash and John East had discovered Elstree in 1913 and decided that it was the ideal location for their new studios, this cinema caption, accompanied by sundry requests like, 'No smoking please, it annoys the ladies'; 'Just a moment please while the operator changes a reel'; and 'Ladies! Kindly remove your hats' were very old hat indeed.

After all, nearly twenty years had elapsed since British film pioneers R.W. Paul, Birt Acres, G.A. Smith, James Williamson and Cecil Hepworth had started the British film exhibition ball rolling into the twentieth century in 1895. Greater London had 600 cinemas by 1913 and studio development

was endeavouring to keep abreast with their growth. Disused skating rinks, gas-works, conservatories and boat-houses – in fact anything that had space and would convert to a glass roof for maximum light, and later, a completely covered one when artificial lighting was introduced – were slowly giving way to purpose-built studios. Fairgrounds, Vaudeville theatres and local halls, used as venues for the travelling film exhibitor, had in turn reverted to their original format, as the first Picture Theatres/Cinemas started to be built in 1908.

Around 1911, film producers might have been happy to hire R.W. Paul's first studio at New Southgate for a guinea a day – it consisted of a mounted stage with sliding doors, the forerunner

OUR VILLAGE CINEMA.

Showman. "'ERE, I SAY, IT BE 'ORSES' 'OOVES, NOT 'ORNS OR 'AIL-STORMS.'"

proved that there was a continuing public demand for film entertainment, film investment was slow to materialise and small producers very often waited many years for their capital return. Nash became convinced that, given the opportunity of setting up a new company where he could control policy, he could produce films economically and quickly to meet the current trends. Courageously, John East agreed to support him and contacted barrister-businessman Arthur Moss Lawrence. Between them they devised a scheme that would attract long term investment. The scheme succeeded and within a short space of time, they found themselves reconnoitering London's green belt, in the hope of finding a fog-free zone which had a good train service to London, beautiful scenery for location work and most important of all, an excellent site for a film studio. They found Elstree, or to be correct they found Borehamwood, an area adjoining the old village of Elstree. But over the decades the British Hollywood was always referred to as Elstree and still is to this day.

Even back in 1910 Elstree seems to have got its

of the present studio stage. Now they wanted sophisticated amenities such as guaranteed artificial lighting, toilet facilities, editing rooms and scenic depots. Unfortunately there were not many of these about. True, Hepworth had the right idea in 1910, with his specially built first-floor stages – with workshops and laboratories underneath – at Walton-on-Thames. But in the main, the transition was a slow one and production facilities were well behind those to be found in America.

In 1913 an actor-manager by the name of John East joined the London Film Company at Twickenham and developed his friendship with colleague Percy Nash. While our early film pioneers had

THE HOME CINEMATOGRAPH FOR SUFFERERS FROM INSOMNIA.

BELOW
The original Neptune Studios at Borehamwood, opened in 1914. Subsequent owners included the Ludwig Blattner Film Corporation and Joe Rock Production. In the mid-thirties the actor Leslie Fuller leased some studio space for several films

priorities right; a former chapel in Gasworks Lane was converted into a small cinema, where for the grand admission fee of 1d, 2d or 3d one could see a varied programme of 'two reelers', 'short comics' and on special days an 'interest feature'. The projector was very aptly illuminated by limelight.

Imaginative as they may have been, the two men standing in the middle of the Hertfordshire countryside in the autumn of 1913, could not have known that they were about to plant a film industry acorn that would grow into a sturdy oak, that would branch out to become the major part of our British film heritage for the next seventy years. What they did know, was that the seven acres they had just purchased were ideal for their needs. With mounting excitement and enthusiasm, and with Arthur Moss Lawrence as the guiding force, the acorn was sown.

Neptune Films was founded in January 1914 and their new studios at Elstree were the finest in England at that time. Purpose-built, they resembled a row of alms-houses rather than a studio, but were cleverly designed to incorporate a pro-

Alf (reading French news). "ALL THE CINEMAS IN CALAIS ARE SHUT UP. MY WORD! THAT BRINGS THE HORRORS OF WAR PRETTY CLOSE HOME!"

jection theatre, dressing rooms with running water, administrative offices, generating plant and processing facilities. The studio (stage) was over seventy feet in length and devoid of glass, claiming the title of the first dark stage in Europe.

Percy Nash was engaged as resident producer at the studios, while John East was to play twin roles: the traditional one of film actor in the Neptune productions and responsibility, with Brian Daly, for script editing, stage adaptations and original screen plays. An excellent P.R. man, East also bought the nearby mansion, Ivy Lodge. He not only lived there, but also used the interior and exterior of the house for a number of films and if the family happened to be around at the same time, then they too would become part of the scenario. It also provided an impressive setting for business meetings and local social gatherings.

With the outbreak of war in 1914, many British films were to take on a patriotic note. But in the main, films were still adapted from popular stage plays and, with foresight and imagination, the studios formed their own stock group of players that included Daisy Cordell, Frank Tennant and Gerald Lawrence. Neptune's first feature, *The Harbour Lights*, was a great success and starred a number of their own players. Well ahead of their time, they obtained the film rights of the works of James Barrie, the most popular piece being *The Little Minister*, which was filmed in 1915.

While almost a generation of British manhood was being devoured as gun fodder in the French trenches, a number of British companies were requested to make government-sponsored recruiting features. Part of Neptune's contribution was *The Royal Naval Division at Work and Play* and *Women in Munitions*. But in the main the theme was escapism with such pieces as *The Romany Rye*, a tale of the family heir turning gipsy to elude the dastardly schemes of his villainous half brother, or *Married for Money*. One had to be sitting comfortably for this one, the saga of a frivolous beauty whose wealthy husband is shot by a 'blinded' fellow, who later poses as a gardener to save the daughter from her influence.

In general the studio prospered splendidly in the first three years, with the permanent company and visiting established artists like stage star Gaby Deslys and May Whitty. Unknown chorus artists like Jack Buchanan were used as extras and paid the daily sum of ten shillings, or one pound if they provided their own evening clothes. It became a point of honour among these artists to be able to smuggle their stage evening clothes out of the theatre, without being caught by the management.

Between 1915 and 1920, Neptune leased or rented their studios to other companies including Ideal Films, and British Lion Film Company (no connection with the later British Lion Films), while British Instructional was to start life in a hut rented to them by Ideal Films. These companies in turn attracted the stage and screen stars of the day, including Ellen Terry, Edith Craig, Denis Neilson Terry, Gladys Cooper, Irene Vanbrugh, Matheson Lang and child actress Fabia Drake, along with many others.

In 1916 the *International Tatler*, the magazine

AN IMPALPABLE FLAME.

Claude. "WHAT ARE YOU WAITIN' HERE FOR, OLD THING?"
Cuthbert. "TO GIVE THESE FLOWERS AND CHOCOLATES TO THAT STUNNING LITTLE GIRL IN 'THE DEATH KISS OF DEADMAN'S GULCH.'"

"I SAY, MAUDE, WE MUST GET DAD TO TAKE US TO THIS. I'VE NEVER SEEN A HOUSE ON FIRE."

devoted to 'International affairs of interest to keen Exhibitors and Live Agents', were to offer their own version of an *Encyclopedia of Trade Terms*.

International Tatler
PAGE SEVEN

ENCYLOPEDIA OF TRADE TERMS.

Film Expert—The man who doesn't know he doesn't know, but thinks he does.

Reviewer—A man who knows he doesn't know but does his best.

Synopsis—A weighty tome like Gibbon's "Roman Empire."

Interior Decorations—Anything in the nature of orange peel, banana skins, nuts shells and cigarette ends.
N.B.—Banana skins strewn in the gangways—all very useful for teaching patrons the " Chaplin act," or " How to earn five millions a minute."

Three Reels—A length of film somewhere between two and four thousand feet.

A Part is equal to its Whole—When no Part One turns up in a Multi-reel feature.

Lead—Something the previous Operator must have removed.

Rain—Welcomed in the Street but not on the Screen.

Bad Joins—The cause of Operator's bad language.

Regulation Film Box—A junior safe-deposit which must be not too large in case it infringes the patents granted to Bank Vaults. It is something like a Zeppelin : you have to sweep up the bits after each trip.

What'll—A popular expression now banned by the Board of Liquor Control.

Date Book—The Manager's Bible. Usually left at the Theatre when he goes out on business.

Foot—There are two kinds : one is the Film Traveller's measurement of length to the Managers ; the other is the Manager's manifestation of the temper to Film Travellers.

Handbills—Things you strew on pavements to prevent people's shoes getting muddy.

Picture Theatres—A useful subject for up-to-date comedians to gag about when stale.

Sub-titles—Wording put in pictures to prompt the amateur critic just when to say " I told you so."

Maltese Cross—Something that makes the Operator get Chinese wild when it sticks.

Racks—The Movie method of eyesight testing.

Contract—Something most Managers are always " coming in to sign."

Flicker—A beautiful " tremolando " effect in Picture projection.

Crossover—When you telephone the Renter about your missing top-liner, and nobody seems to know anything ; that's what you get " cross over."

Change Days—The days when Operators collect small change.

Arc Lamp—A method of illumination used by Noah during the flood.

Carbons—Things as difficult to corner as the circle is to square.

Judgment—Something you say *you* have when you put one over the *other man*.

Luck—Something you say the *other man* has when he puts one over on *you*.

Modesty—Twin Brother to the Dodo in film advertising.

Truth—Something you must not show to the public (*vide* " Hypocrites.")

Patience—Something that deserts you when your top-liner fails to report.

Opposition—Something that is sent to try us.

Weather—An obstinate brute who delights in contradicting the experts.

Democrat—The man who says it's *Cinema*.

Plutocrat—The man who says it's *Kinema*.

Is it likely we should recommend you an inferior article ? "International-Litchfield Street."

The Picture House, Falkirk

LEFT
Ludwig Blattner, proprietor of the Neptune Studios in 1928, seen here with his son Gerry and actress Ellen Terry. Blattner developed the *Blattnerphone*, the first known commercial electro-magnetic sound recording machine wire and tape

The Plaza, Wishaw

The Ritz, Cambuslang

"No. No. NO! That's not the way to die! Put more life into it."

But the war was to take its toll, not only of young lives, but of British film technicians and artists, and the introduction of an Amusement Tax caused a loss at the box office. Added to this, American films flooded the home market and the British producer became more and more the victim of circumstance. Neptune was forced to cease production in 1917 and further difficulties compelled them to mortgage two-thirds of their land in 1918.

In 1920 the company went into liquidation and by August 1921, it was all over. For a time Ideal Films leased the premises and in 1928, Ludwig Blattner bought the studios and the Blattner Film Corporation was formed. Another Elstree studio was to be opened in that year, the Whitehall Studios, later to be known as the Gate Studios. They were headed by Adelqui Millar as Managing Director and Chief Producer.

At the time of Neptune's demise in 1920, industry training was something that one achieved by accident rather than design, and certainly more than one American producer – like the one who hoped to found a British Los Angeles at Bournemouth – contemplated the expansion of the British studios, along with its weak home market.

Although by 1924 nearly every British studio was closed, the Elstree acorn planted in 1913 had grown, with a shoot that was clearly visible in Neptune's achievements.

In 1925, American film entrepreneur J.D. Williams came, saw, and was conquered. Bournemouth could cry its heart out, for he decided there and then that he would make Elstree, the British Hollywood.

Chapter 2

Entry of the Gladiators

Harriet Hi!
Light of my eye!
Come to the Pictures and have a good cry,
For it's jolly old Saturday,
Mad-as-a-hatter-day,
Nothing-much-matter-day-night.

From *Saturday Night* by Sir Alan P. Herbert.

'British Producers Handicapped.

At the moment of writing there are very few British pictures
being made. Many causes are responsible for this lamentable
state of affairs, but one of the chief handicaps under which our
producers have had to labour is lack of financial backing.
American bankers saw great possibilities of the cinema industry
and fostered it, but in England the men with money have always
been scared of putting capital into the industry.'

From *Picture Show*, 1926.

MANY studios have come and gone at Elstree since the early silent film days. They all sparkled brightly in their own right and in time fell sadly to earth. The B.I.P. studios, now Thorn-EMI Elstree Studios Ltd, are the sole survivors of Elstree's British Hollywood and with the exception of most of the war years (1940–45), when it became an army garrison theatre and depot, have been making films since the mid-twenties. Over half a century of British film making.

British International Pictures Ltd, known affectionately as the 'Porridge Factory' or the 'Associated Scottish', was founded by John Maxwell and commenced business on March 31st 1927, with a share capital of £50,000. The British

film industry will always owe a debt of gratitude to this canny, clever Scot who had the vision and the courage to invest his skills and money in the pursuit of its development.

The building of the studios was, in fact, begun and almost completed by American film pioneer J.D. Williams. He had formed British National Films with W. Schlesinger and invited Herbert Wilcox into the company. In 1925, they bought forty acres of land at Elstree with a view to building studios comparable to those in Hollywood. They succeeded, but discord soon arose between Williams and Schlesinger. The conflict developed into litigation and John Maxwell, already a respected member of the industry, was called in. He provided finance and gained control of the company and the studio.

Having lost a considerable amount of his own money, J.D. Williams returned to the States and after a short time Herbert Wilcox left to partner top musical star of the twenties Nelson Keys in the founding of a new film company, the British and Dominions Film Corporation. Mr Wilcox did not have to travel too far afield for this new venture. The B. and D. Film Corporation leased studios from John Maxwell that adjoined the British International Pictures – the studios that Wilcox had helped J.D. Williams to build.

Maxwell, a Glasgow solicitor, had already been in the film business for fifteen years by the time he founded B.I.P. in 1927. A cautious gentleman, he had been surprised to discover from his accountant

RIGHT
J. D. Williams (left) and Herbert Wilcox in 1926

BELOW
The B.I.P. Studios. Built in 1925–6 by J. D. Williams, W. Schlesinger and Herbert Wilcox and named British National Studios, they were acquired in 1927 by John Maxwell, who changed the name to British International Pictures

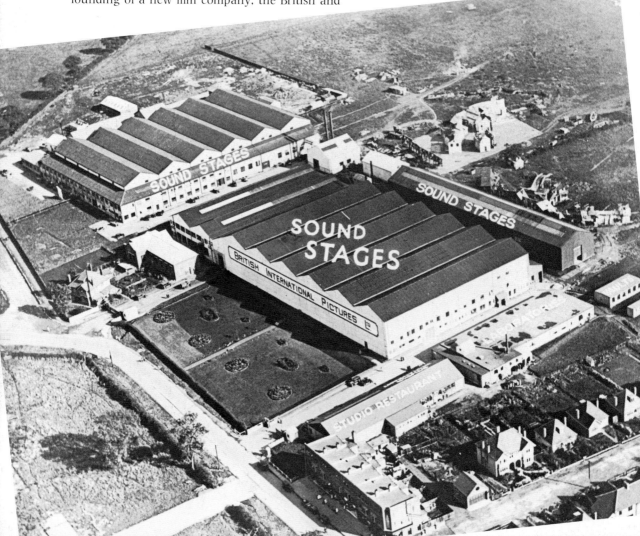

Nelson Keys (left), Dorothy Gish and Will Rogers.
Herbert Wilcox formed the British and Dominions Film
Corporation with Keys and used all three artists in a
number of his productions

in 1912 that he had interests in the 'cinema theatre
business'. Be that as it may, no stretch of the
imagination could confuse his conception of a
British film studio with accident, rather than
design and a long careful study of the industry.

After his initial interest in 'exhibiting', he went
on to take part in the founding of Waverley Films, a
Scottish distributing company, which handled the
pictures of Wardour Films of London. Some time
later he acquired Wardour Films itself and trans-
formed it from a minor concern into a major film
renting house.

Maxwell soon realised, however, that the role of

the British exhibitor and renter, without a guaranteed supply of American product, was far from
easy and that the future lay in the formation
of a combined producing/distributing/exhibiting
framework, with a large British studio as its
foundation stone.

His decision was no doubt nudged by the
knowledge that the Federation of British Industries
had inaugurated a campaign to secure statutory
protection for the British film-producing industry.
Indeed the government introduced the Cinematograph Films Bill in April 1927, only a month after
Maxwell opened the B.I.P. studios. The Bill stipulated that the cinemas would be called upon to
include in their programmes a proportion of British
films, rising to twenty per cent; while film renters
were required to obtain a similar percentage of
British films for distribution. The Bill became law in
December, 1927.

Although Herbert Wilcox had christened the new studios with his production of *Madame Pompadour* with the unique Dorothy Gish in the name part, the first film under the new B.I.P. banner was *The White Sheik* in 1927. Former beauty queen Lillian Hall-Davis and heart-throb Warwick Ward played the passionate, if silent, lovers. She was to fade out of films some years later; he was to go on to make a further career as Production and Studio Manager and much later, in 1948, to make the company's 250th film *My Brother Jonathan*.

There was, of course, no sound track in those days. If the scenario was not going too well, major changes to the story could easily be effected by a quick reshuffle of film sections already in the 'can'. None of the artists on location in Morocco for *The White Sheik* had a script; instead, they were given the story line on a verbal, day-to-day basis and the story underwent constant changes until the film was almost complete.

Betty Balfour, known as the English Mary Pickford and pin-up of thousands, followed the Moroccan adventure with *A Little Bit Of Fluff*. So popular was this lady, that when the studios staged a publicity stunt and advertised for a bodyguard, they received 500 male applicants. Why, with that number to choose from, they should have assigned her a bow-legged 'heavy', is a matter for speculation.

Although scene stealers in their own right, animals were not accorded the same star status as Miss Balfour. In those early days the unfortunate creatures would be transported from London in uncomfortable conditions and without handlers. They would arrive in humours that were far from accommodating, and it often took a certain ingenuity on the part of the studio manager to cope with the situation. On arrival at the studio an out-of-work boilerman was told that all he had to do was to look after the animals 'in case they got thirsty'. He signed off five minutes later with, 'If them lions want a drink they can get it themselves.'

Dorothy Gish (front, left) in *Madame Pompadour*, 1927

Marie Ault in *The Silver Lining*, with Pat Aherne as her son, wrongfully convicted of the robbery committed by his brother

The continuity girl on the Betty Balfour film *A Little Bit Of Fluff* ended up with just that: a dog, which was to be her house guest until the completion of filming, when it was presented to her by the star – she christened it Betty.

From the inception of B.I.P., John Maxwell had planned that it should become an international organisation, its very name reflecting the scope of its activities. He set to work to surround himself with people he felt could understand this concept, whether they be in front of the cameras or behind them. Accordingly, in 1927, after *Poppies of Flanders*, directed by Arthur Maude, starring Jameson Thomas and Eve Gray, and *The Silver Lining* with Pat Aherne and John Hamilton, he acquired the services of a twenty-eight-year-old director called Alfred Hitchcock for a three-year, twelve-picture contract at £13,000 a year. Mr Hitchcock came from a modest background and had started his career in the film industry as a handyman at Islington Studios, and the shrewd Mr Maxwell obviously recognised his potential.

Hitchcock's first film for Maxwell was *The Ring*, starring the Danish actor Carl Brisson and Lillian Hall-Davis. It was a story of boxing rings and fair grounds and was shot by B.I.P.'s Director of Photography, Jack Cox.

The Ring, and Hitchcock in particular, received excellent notices; the *Bioscope* called it 'The most magnificent British film ever made,' while the *Morning Post* was to announce '. . . . . . Had I to demonstrate to the most hardened disbeliever in British films the essential vitality of the industry, I should take him to the British International Studios at Elstree.'

John Maxwell's next move was to appoint Walter Mycroft, a founder member of the London Film Society and film critic of the *Evening Standard*, first as scenario editor and then as head of the studios. Mycroft, a hunchback, always attended by a retinue of employees, was a man of such authority and striking appearance that he became known as 'Czar of all the Rushes'. Although Hitchcock was to announce that he managed to make films 'in spite of Mycroft' this unlikely pair, with an incredible eye for detail and effect, held each other in remarkable esteem.

By 1928, J.D. Williams, who had fled to the

RIGHT
Lillian Hall-Davis, Jameson Thomas and Gordon Harker (left) in another Hitchcock film, *The Farmer's Wife* – a tale of a widowed farmer in search of a wife

BELOW
It's a knock-out: the recipient is Ian Hunter in Alfred Hitchcock's *The Ring*

States on the collapse of the funding of the original studio building, had made a tenacious re-entry into the British film industry, albeit at a distance. He had become a Director of the World Wide Pictures Corporation, a newly formed company which was to market B.I.P. productions in the United States. Maxwell had also bought the German company Sudfilm to make films for B.I.P. in Germany and to distribute for them.

Not Quite a Lady, directed by Thomas Bentley, with Mabel Poulton, Barbara Gott and Maurice Bradell, and *The Farmer's Wife*, with Hitchcock directing and starring Jameson Thomas and Lillian Hall-Davis, were the next fillies to be trotted out of the Maxwell stable. Owner Maxwell moved on at a

RIGHT
Beautiful Maria Corda getting married to heart-throb Jameson Thomas in *Tesha*

BELOW
Beautiful Maria Corda after her marriage to heart-throb Jameson Thomas in *Tesha*

'Don't ring us, we'll ring you': Betty Balfour in Hitchcock's *Champagne*

rare gallop; if his 'British Hollywood' was to become a total reality, then the only way to make economic productions and sound marketing sense was to secure distribution abroad (which he was already negotiating) and to use American and to a lesser extent German stars.

Producers Herbert Wilcox and Michael Balcon were rapidly coming to the same conclusion. They were equally aware that Hollywood was enticing many of the British stars to their shores, including Brian Aherne, Ralph Forbes, John Loder, Victor McLaglen, Ray Milland and Madeleine Carroll. So, the British Hollywood in the twenties decided on its own version of *Star Wars*.

Over the following years Maxwell was to invite Maria Corda, Syd Chaplin, Antonio Moreno and Olga Tschechowa, Tallulah Bankhead, Lionel Barrymore, Anna May Wong, Monty Banks, Gilda

Gray and many others over from the States to appear in his pictures. Wilcox attracted Betty Blythe, Dorothy Gish and Will Rogers, while Balcon lured Betty Compson over for his first productions with handsome cash incentives.

Slowly but surely, the structure of Maxwell's organisation was taking shape. In 1928 he gained control of First National-Pathe Ltd., whose main occupation was to deal with the distribution of the many important productions of First National Pictures, Inc., of U.S.A. in Great Britain and also to distribute a number of B.I.P. 'Quota Quickies' to comply with the Cinematograph Films Act.

While Hitchcock continued to fulfil his contract with *Champagne* in 1928, with Betty Balfour, Gordon Harker, Ferdinand von Alten and others, director Victor Saville was making his first film for Maxwell, *Tesha* with Maria Corda, who had recently returned from her American appearance in *Helen of Troy*. Maxwell had formed Burlington Films, a private company, and invited Saville from

Alexandre D'Arcy (in leopard skin) was hailed as Valentino's successor and rushed to England to star in *Paradise*. He is seen here with co-star Betty Balfour

Gainsborough Pictures to be its Managing Director and make films at the B.I.P. studios. As was customary in the silent days, two companies could work at once on the huge barn-like stages and on this occasion it was Saville at one end and the 'Boy Wonder', as he called Hitchcock, at the other. Saville's many films for Maxwell included *Kitty* and *The W Plan*.

There was, of course, always the odd miscalculation in the industry. Because the film act of 1927 stipulated that cinemas had to include a twenty per cent British quota in their programme, many 'Quota Quickies' (often inferior B movies) were churned out to comply with this ruling, with an eye to box office receipts rather than artistic integrity.

Director Denison Clift discovered a strikingly handsome young French-Egyptian actor, playing a small part in a French studio. His name was Alexandre D'Arcy and he bore a striking resemblance to Rudolf Valentino. D'Arcy was rushed to England, hailed as the 'Great Lover's' successor and given the lead in Clift's *Paradise* with Betty Balfour, Winter Hall and Joseph Striker. A vigorous publicity campaign announced that he was the 'film actor with the world at his feet'; but this fervour was short-lived. Whether it was the sight of his brilliantined locks making a mockery of his leopard skin or the unenthusiastic manner with

which he shoved their beloved Miss Balfour through the studio's best Paradise foliage, we may never know. All that we do know for certain is that he was box office poison.

The famous comedian/director Monty Banks was also to make a casting error a few years later. Having tested, without success, many young actresses to play his fiancee in his next film comedy *The Compulsory Husband*, he had all but given up in despair when on a visit to the theatre he espied a lovely young maiden – selling programmes. Without further ado and in truly romantic fashion he signed her up on the spot and swept his unblemished rose off to the studios. She did extremely well in the film and a glamorous new career lay before her. There were, however, two points to be taken into consideration, that she had omitted to mention. She was married – and she was pregnant. At the end of the filming she returned to her original role, that of a happy suburban housewife. Her name was Lillian Manton.

***

Never a flamboyant figure, Maxwell nevertheless decided that the time had come for a certain display of showmanship, and possibly one-upmanship, with his 1928 trade showing of *Moulin Rouge*.

Victor Saville directed Estelle Brody and John Stuart in *Kitty*

Olga Tschechowa in
Moulin Rouge

It was his biggest film venture to date. With Hitchcock and Saville already under contract, he invited E.A. Dupont, the eminent German director of *Vaudeville*, to direct this enterprise. The Russian actress, Olga Tschechowa and the French actor, Jean Bradin, were to star.

Dupont, an extraordinarily gifted man who was to go on to direct *Piccadilly* and *Atlantic*, could display more temperament in ten minutes, than a studio of stars in ten years. He adored his little 'production touches' and hated working in the morning. Both of these little foibles were to cost John Maxwell, who had personally invested in the film, a lot of money. The 'touches', while original and prestigious, were extremely costly and his brunchtime start to the day meant that he preferred to work on until after midnight, if necessary – to the delight of his sleep-starved workers of all grades, who were on overtime.

A director of immense vision, with a wonderful capacity for handling his artistes, he undoubtedly brought a continental glamour and esteem to our

ABOVE
Gladys Frazin with her real-life husband Monty Banks in *The Compulsory Husband*

BELOW
Lillian Hall-Davis and Henry Victor in *Tommy Atkins*

films; but in those early days, when John Maxwell was struggling for production supremacy and with *Moulin Rouge* already exceeding its £80,000 budget (a vast sum in those days), the thrifty Scot might have been forgiven for wondering if this was an expensive luxury that he could ill afford. Nevertheless, the *Daily Mirror* was to say that *Moulin Rouge* was the 'most sensational film yet to be made by a British company, . . . brilliant technique'.

Matinee idol Jack Buchanan, who was to delight and thrill his audiences for several decades to come with his elegant musical comedy routines, starred next in *Toni*, a dual role, with Dorothy Boyd, Moore Marriott playing an international crook and Arthur Maude directing. On its heels came *Tommy Atkins* which had its trade show in 1928 to public acclaim.

By 1928, a new breed of young screen heroes – like Jack Buchanan, Brian Aherne, John Longden – had emerged to replace the pre-war favourites, but leading and supporting actors were still, in the main, recruited from the stage. Actors like Ivor Novello, Fay Compton and Owen Nares wisely decided to keep a foot in both camps to ensure an eventual entree to the Hollywood Hollywood from the British Hollywood.

Meantime the 'legit' theatre folk did not mention their film work too much. It was after all something one did for the money rather than one's art.

One young lady, still unbothered by this dilemma but who was to spend a number of years at Elstree at the adjoining B. and D. studios, was one of 'Mr Cochran's Young Ladies'. Nevertheless, in his revue early in 1929, in which Jessie Matthews and Sonnie Hale were 'wowing them in the aisles' with numbers like *Let's Do It*, the lovely Marjorie Robertson must have had that certain feeling that her big break was soon to come. With it came a change of name – Anna Neagle was to be her choice.

After *Tommy Atkins*, Monty Banks and Gillian Dean starred in *Adam's Apple* and while the established *Bioscope* and *Kineweekly* looked on, *Film Weekly*, a new British independent film newspaper, price 2d, had its first publication in 1928.

While its copy was geared to industry articles and trade advertisements, such as a double pro-

Once one of 'Mr Cochran's Young Ladies', Anna Neagle is pictured here in *The Chinese Bungalow*

gramme at the Plaza, Piccadilly with *Poppies of Flanders* and Bebe Daniels in *Take Me Home* 'dedicated to the chorus girl, often in tight situations!', plus Albert Sandler and the Plaza Symphony Orchestra, *On the Stage* (one wonders where else they might have been), it was clear from the non-film publicity and market research of the day that the publishers had a fairly clear idea as to their future readership.

'Boneless Bontonettes and Brevity Sets, in Milanese or Stockinette worn next to the skin?' 'Exquisite garments of gossamer loveliness . . . . with moulded bust, 39/6d.' 'To possess teeth as pearly white as Miss Laura La Plante's . . . . . use ODOL'. Add 'A Menu Of The Moment', involving three pounds of fresh salmon, and comforting articles like 'Do Film Producers Understand Women,' and 'Man's Dangerous Age' and they had more or less given the game away. It should be noted that the price of a mid-day matinee seat for Leicester Square Photo Play was 1/3d, tax 3d.

While John Maxwell might have been amused by the copy, his aim was the same as that of the new *Film Weekly*, to get the public into the cinemas. He did after all own a great many of them by this time. In 1928, he formed a subsidiary company of B.I.P., Associated British Cinemas Ltd. It started with forty cinemas and by 1930 had grown to 120 theatres. The chain extended throughout the British Isles and included some of the most modern – and for those days – glamorous houses in the country, including the Regal, Marble Arch and the Lido, Golders Green. This was a direct challenge to the Gaumont group, who by 1929 had 280 cinemas in their circuit as well as an interest, like Maxwell, in production and distribution.

As the silent era drew to a close, the film industry became conscious that two Goliaths were emerging and that one of them would probably succeed to the role of David. They were John Maxwell for A.B.C and C.M. Woolf for Gaumont-British.

Harry Lachman, a former associate of director Rex Ingram and an assistant at the Nice studios, had also caught the eye of Maxwell. In 1927 he became Studio Technical Advisor for B.I.P. and then went on to direct *Week-End Wives* starring Monty Banks, Annette Benson and Estelle Brody. Estelle had come to England to appear in a stage play and remained to soar to stardom in the British Hollywood and become known as 'the comic Clara Bow'.

Widecombe Fair, with Wyndham Standing as the

BELOW: The Regal, Marble Arch.   BELOW RIGHT: The Lido, Golders Green

ABOVE
Harry Lachman (seated) directing *Weekend Wives*.
Around him (left to right) are cameraman Jack Cox,
F. W. Ewing, Jameson Thomas and smiling Estelle
Brody, known as the comic Clara Bow

ABOVE
Piccadilly: a famous quartet in 1929. From left to right, producer/director E. A. Dupont, Arnold Bennett (who wrote the original story), Gilda Gray and Jameson Thomas

RIGHT
Anna May Wong in *Piccadilly*, 1929

Squire and Marguerite Allen as his daughter, and *Emerald of the East* were to follow; the latter starred French actress Mary Odette and a 'six-year-old' Kenneth Rive (later head of Gala Films) playing the Maharajah's son.

It is difficult to surmise whether the British Board of Film Censors in 1929 were alerted to the possible dangers to public morals by the brave Lieutenant Desmond Armstrong (Joshua Kean) and the Maharanee (Lya Delvelez) in *Emerald of the East* or by Moore Marriot's interpretation of Uncle Tom Cobleigh in *Widecombe Fair*. Suffice it to say that its report made quite clear its 'reasons for exception being taken to certain productions'. They were:

1. Reflection on Wife of responsible British Official stationed in the East.
2. Police firing on defenceless populace.
3. Incidents which convey false and derogatory impressions of the Police Force in this country.
4. Intimate biological studies unsuitable for general exhibition.

The 'flapper's delight' Carl Brisson (left) with Malcolm Keen and Anny Ondra in Hitchcock's *The Manxman*

5. Unseemly display of woman's undergarments.
6. Crude immorality.
7. Women in alluring and provocative attitudes.
8. Men and Women in bed together.
9. Inflammatory sub-titles and political propaganda.

Charles Laughton had his first day's film work as a 'continental visitor' in Arnold Bennett's *Piccadilly*, the now famous Dupont film of 1929. He was to go on to stardom in the title role in Sir Alexander Korda's *Private Life of Henry VIII* at Herbert Wilcox's studio next door.

Piccadilly, the story of London life, night clubs and slums, provided the background for the drama which starred Gilda Gray, the delightful Chinese actress Anna May Wong – as 'Shosho', the scullion who becomes a star – and Jameson Thomas, whom Dupont described as 'the finest actor in England'. With a German director and Chinese, English and Polish-American stars, John Maxwell must have been well pleased with such an ambitious international line-up, if not with Dupont's equally ambitious budget.

In 1928 and 1929 a feeling of trepidation was beginning to take hold in the corridors of power in Wardour Street. It stemmed from one word, *sound*.

Ernest Betts writing on *Why Talkies Are Unsound*, (no pun intended) said 'Put speech into films and you will get speech plus film, but you will not get a film.' Hugh Castle wrote, '. . . And Talkies? *No*, it is too much . . .' and in July of 1929 was to add, 'The home product is feeling unwell. Rumour has it that it is busy finding its voice. One can but hope that it will die dumb.'

Whatever anxieties John Maxwell might have had, the hardy Scot kept them to himself and ended the silent era with a trade showing in December 1928 of *The Manxman*, starring 'the flapper's delight', Carl Brisson and directed by Alfred Hitchcock; and *Cocktails*, directed by Monty Banks with Pat and Patachon as 'Gin and It'! In February of 1929, *The Lily of Killarney* adapted from the stage play *The Colleen Bawn* and directed by George Ridgwell, was given its premiere.

From the presentation of *The White Sheik* in 1927 to the introduction of talkies, Maxwell had produced or invested in twenty-four feature films at Elstree – no mean achievement. Two years earlier Maxwell's film interests had been confined to exhibition and distribution; now he was a major producer and studio owner. In the latter part of 1929 he acquired the services of a young Scotsman fresh from Glasgow University, for his law practice, then invited him into the London office. Robert Clark was to participate in the history and success of Maxwell's studios for the next forty years and eventually become his very admirable successor.

Change was inevitable; the real struggle for British film and studio supremacy was about to begin, but John Maxwell was perfectly capable of accepting that challenge.

Chapter 3
Sounding Off

Don't need the Joanna no more,
Or Coconut shells for gallopin' gees,
No wind screen naw to cut me fingers sore,
Real bleedin' rain!
Won't need me tin of dried up peas!

Cinema Pianist's Lament.

The Future.   A selection of practical management.

Sound and colour place a direct strain on two human senses
almost every hour of every normal day and to encounter them in
one's entertainment might prove anything but a relaxation. In
the theatre and music-hall the appeal is made naturally through
real people and real colour, whereas in the cinema we are
entertained by illusion – the shadow taking the place of
substance . . . Thus it may be taken that the silent *black and*
white film will remain the stable product of the industry while
sound, colour and stereoscopy will remain items of novel *appeal.*

The Bioscope Service Supplement, 1928.

SCEPTICISM partnered by fear in 1927/28 triggered off a dozen or more financial, practical and artistic reasons why sound could not succeed – from Warwick Deeping writing in *The Film Weekly* in 1928:
'. . . . And what sort of voice will it be? Again we are forced to consider the contrasts of the stage. I could listen to Edith Evans for hours, but God forbid that I should have to listen to a moving picture of Edith Evans addressing me through some mechanism' – to the novel approach of a worried Cinema Manager from Gloucester:
'. . . . . What about patrons afflicted by deafness who number thousands? In spite of wonderful appliances of which I have personal experience, none of them efficiently give the afflicted one

that which has been lost.' (*The Bioscope*, 1928.)
Whether one should deduce from this plea not only that the gentleman was stone deaf, but that he had recently lost his ear trumpet is just one interpretation open to the reader.
If the British public bought a weekly film paper, during this period, they would know that there were less than a hundred 'Talkie Theatres' in the country, of which very few were in the provinces. With the heavy financial risk for studios and cinemas alike attached to the cost of installation, the cinema owners' attitude was understandably one of extreme caution.
Five main recording systems had emerged. Movietone had the sound recorded on a narrow strip at the side of the pictorial film; Vitaphone

operated with a synchronised gramophone record: British Acoustic had two films – one for the sound recess; Blattner made use of sensitised wire; while Phonofilm was identical in principle to Movietone.

The Audible Pictures Ltd. Han-A-Phone system was brought before the public as an investment proposition of £250,000 in two-shilling shares in 1928. This was a disc recording sound amplification method which had been successfully demonstrated in London. But the industry remained cautious. *The Film Weekly* urged that 'Investors should not rush', as other similar systems would very soon be on the market.

Not a man to rush into anything, John Maxwell had been quietly preparing the ground for the eventuality of the success of sound. It arrived with a bang, with Warner Brothers' Vitaphone (sound on disc) production of *The Jazz Singer* starring Al Jolson, in 1927. The following year Maxwell's box office tills tinkled merrily from the queues surrounding his recently opened Regal cinema at Marble Arch. The attraction was Warner's *The Singing Fool*, again starring Al Jolson, the first American major sound feature film to be presented in London. By this time, Maxwell had already despatched John Thorpe, his general manager, to America, with orders to purchase sound equipment, cameras and expertise – proving that yet again he was prepared to put his personal fortune where his mouth was.

There was now fierce competition to be first with a British sound feature. With the added complication of different recording systems and trade show dates, there were many conflicting claims. Herbert Wilcox with *Wolves*; British Sound Films with *The Crimson Circle* and Neo-Art Productions' *White Cargo*. Certainly Britain's first *all-talking* feature was *The Clue of the New Pin*, produced by British Lion, in which a young actor named John Gielgud had a tiny part. But Alfred Hitchcock's *Blackmail*, made for John Maxwell's B.I.P. at Elstree, is usually regarded by the industry as Britain's entry into sound film production.

Maxwell's efforts to gather together as much expert knowledge as possible in a very short time including tempting two accomplished men to join him from the B.B.C. were successful. R.E. Jeffrey had extensive experience of sound recording and studio construction, and D.F. Scanlan had been one of the chief engineers at 2LO. Work commenced at B.I.P. in April 1929 on two temporary sound studios, and under the supervision of Jeffrey

Stars John Longden and Anny Ondra in a scene from *Blackmail*

and Scanlan, R.C.A. Photophone recording equipment was installed. The building materials constructed an excellent case for a pyromaniac's paradise. The timber framework was lined with celotex, a fibrous composition of crushed sugar cane, and the interior walls were draped with heavy flannelette. A coconut fibre covered the floor, to deaden sound.

It was in these primitive conditions, then, before the permanent sound stages were ready, working on a film that had been half completed as a silent movie and having to cope with all the new problems relating to cameras and acting techniques, that the hardy Hitch, backed and nudged on by Maxwell, commenced his first talkie production, *Blackmail*.

Years later Dick Cavett was to say that 'Movies are full of people who project a mysterious something on the screen – that is entirely absent when you meet them.' For talkies that 'something' also had to have a voice, and the casualties are now legendary. Anny Ondra, the lovely star of *Blackmail*, whose films had sold well in the States and in Europe with a silent passport, found her bank balance whittling away at an alarming rate the moment that she opened her mouth. Her thick Czech accent and the early recording systems in that temporary studio joined forces to give her adoring public a totally incomprehensible noise. As post-dubbing was not possible at that time,

English actress Joan Barry dubbed the star's voice, by reading Miss Ondra's lines into a microphone as the lady was performing – a feat which also earned *Blackmail* the title of 'The first British film to be dubbed'.

Suitable voice tone and diction apart, the actor's lot was not a happy one with the advent of sound. The expression 'starched shirt' acquired a new meaning when it was discovered that this was the culprit responsible for the 'newspaper tearing' sounds on the new recordings. Shadows cast by bulky microphones might have been fine for *Mimi*, to be made a couple of years later, but not for the non-consumptive heroines – and at some British studios, these ladies suffered from unsightly rashes due to powdered glass (used to fill the soundproof walls) being wafted over them through the ventilators.

New sound studios at Elstree: on the set for the B.I.P. film *Blackmail*

To find a voice was one thing, to find that you hadn't got one was even worse, but perhaps the real tragedy was for the silent film comedian, whose art could never be the same again.

An actor's free range movement was now at an end. It had to be, because three feet above or three steps ahead was a static microphone concealed in the set decoration. An actor moved, delivered and cut. Even for a director of Hitchcock's inventive ability, the necessity of moving the actors to deliver stilted lines into yet another bowl of fruit or up a chimney must have become exhausting and put acting styles back to the early silent period. With sound effects and music at the beginning of the film, it was not until *Blackmail* was into its second reel that the actors were able to get the plot under way. Hitch was to comment, 'The only thing wrong with silent film was the fact that people opened their mouths and no sound came out'; and of drama, 'What is drama but life with the dull bits cut out?' With *Blackmail* he was in a position to justify both these statements. The story is based

on a 'dreadful play' about a detective who is black-mailed, when he withholds information concerning his girlfriend, who has murdered an artist.

Blackmail was premiered at Maxwell's Marble Arch cinema in June 1929, just one year after America's first major sound feature success at the same venue. It was a tremendous success. The publicity and posters shrieked: 'See It and Hear It – Our Mother Tongue As It Should Be Spoken', copy that must have gladdened the heart and bank account of any British voice coach.

Had Hitchcock been German the critics would no doubt have hailed him as a genius. As it was they were quick to point out his 'continental touches': a 'pull back' from the wheel of a Flying Squad car until the camera runs parallel to the vehicle; a staircase shot with tilted camera, and so on.

***

There were two new faces on the B.I.P. stages at this time, a 'clapper boy' (a new job necessary to talkies) by the name of Ronald Neame, and a stills

photographer called Michael Powell. By the time the young Duke and Duchess of York, later King George VI and Queen Elizabeth, had visited the *Blackmail* set, these two now eminent gentlemen probably realised that 'sound' was the voice of the future.

John Maxwell pressed on with two 'quota quickies', *The Flying Scotsman* and *The Lady from the Sea*, which featured a young actor, Reginald Truscott-Jones. He did not, as the old joke goes, change his name to Alfred Truscott-Jones, but to Ray Milland. The next B.I.P. major production was to become an archive classic: *Atlantic*, the first talkie produced in different language versions, was

A Czech accent and the early recording systems joined forces during the filming of *Blackmail* to give Anny Ondra's public a totally incomprehensible noise – Joan Barry was called in to dub the star's voice. Here an anxious Hitchcock, on set with Anny Ondra, tests for sound quality

45

Welsh-born Reginald Truscott-Jones became a great favourite in Britain and Hollywood as Ray Milland

Madeleine Carroll and John Stuart in *Atlantic*

released with separate English, French and German sound-tracks. There were two extras in this film who were to become stars, Michael Wilding and Jimmy Stewart; due to the fact that another actor with the same name had already become a star, Jimmy changed his name to Stewart Granger. If Wilding and Granger were handsome, fellow extra Terry Thomas was dapper. Robert Lennard, later to become casting director of the studios, always felt obliged to pay him more than the others because of his immaculate appearance.

Directed by E.A. Dupont, *Atlantic* starred John Longden and Donald Calthrop, with Monty Banks in a supporting role; and in a tiny part, a former school teacher whose cool English beauty was to take her to international stardom, Madeleine Carroll. While the film, which was based on the *Titanic* tragedy, undoubtedly had much to recommend it, the slowness of the scene in which the captain breaks the news to a wheel-chair-bound passenger that the ship is going down, has singled itself out as an all time classic.

To lighten the drama and now considered respectable enough to attend the theatrical 'high day' Garden Party, albeit through their own Film Artists' Guild, most of the cast decided to raise funds for charity by making capital out of polygamy, bigamy and worse. With Tubby Phillips, the twenty-six stone B.I.P. comedian in the role of 'Smithy-cleric', they set up a 'Film Stars' Gretna Green', where any member of the public willing to pay one shilling would be issued with a tram-ticket-type marriage certificate. While the film actors may not have set quite the required tone for this refined event, they undoubtedly made a 'bomb' for the charity.

Former amateur lightweight boxing champion and dancer Carl Brisson certainly needed to be on his toes for Maxwell's next production, *The American Prisoner*, the story of an American prisoner of war, who escapes to rescue a damsel in distress. The damsel in question: Madeleine Carroll, who had gained speedy promotion to the part of the Squire's daughter.

The American Prisoner was directed by the distinguished Thomas Bentley. Bentley would arrive on set in a Panama hat with a megaphone hanging

RIGHT
The Duke and Duchess of York, later King George VI and Queen Elizabeth, visiting the *Blackmail* set. On the left, the now-legendary studio manager, Joe Grossman

from his neck alongside a spy-glass – an ingenious affair on a little brass tripod, through which he would squint at the set. The electricians christened him 'Shilling-round-the-island'.

Bentley's next film at Elstree was the first British talkie to be released in colour, *Harmony Heaven* with Polly Ward and Stuart Hall. This was followed by Alfred Hitchcock's production of *Juno and the Paycock*, which was not an outstanding success. Hitch seems to have misread the emotions of his audiences and the dramatic undercurrents of Sean O'Casey's play. Edward Chapman and Sara Allgood starred.

While cinema owners were increasingly delighted with the larger audiences that talkies were attracting, they, like the actors and technicians, were encountering problems. Sound equipment meant heavy financial outlay and renters no longer supplied them with films for a simple hiring charge: they now wanted a percentage of the box office takings and a stipulated minimum payment. Cinema owners were also irked by the fact that, while it was illegal to visit a cinema in most parts of the country on a Sunday, pub owners were able to run film shows for their patrons, seven days a week. Licensees were to play a similar hand many years later with a screen that was small enough to sit on their counters.

***

Feared and respected as he might have been, Walter Mycroft undoubtedly had the same eye for talent that was second nature to John Maxwell. This gifted and dedicated man had three men on his B.I.P. payroll in 1929 who were to become known throughout the industry for their scenario work: Val Valentine, Sidney Gilliat and Frank Launder. While the young Launder worked on his first script *Under the Greenwood Tree*, which had been made as a silent film, Mycroft received many unsolicited scripts from a cross-section of the general public, including an ultra-sophisticated one from a clergyman, about a trial marriage, that no censor would have passed.

After *Alf's Carpet*, a comedy directed by W.P.

Popular comedian of the day Leslie Fuller made a number of films at the B.I.P. Studios. He is seen here in charge of the Sheik's harem in *Why Sailors Leave Home*, directed by Monty Banks

ABOVE
Nobby (Donald Calthrop) illustrates to members of his staff how Carl (Carl Brisson) saved his life in the Foreign Legion in *Song of Soho*

TOP
Carl Brisson and Edna Davies in *Song of Soho*

Kellino, B.I.P. decided to make *The Song of Soho*, the story of a young singer wrongly accused of murder, whose innocence is proved when a blind beggar hears him sing in court. Carl Brisson, Edna Davies and Donald Calthrop starred.

At this time, with something of a financial crisis at B.I.P., the publicity department was closed and young Frank Launder given the job in addition to his screenwriting. He decided to impress the management with this act of confidence, and printed a thousand ten-by-eight topless poses of Chinese actress Anna May Wong, who was working at Elstree at the time. These he distributed throughout the world. He was removed from office shortly afterwards, 'financial reasons' being given by way

of explanation. The canny Scots accountancy had not exactly misfired, however – it was Launder's status that had been promoted, albeit temporarily – not his salary.

Collecting yet another first for Elstree, John Maxwell produced 'the first British Film Musical', *Raise the Roof*, starring the ever-popular Betty Balfour, Maurice Evans and Jack Raine. It told the story of a wealthy father who bribes the actress of a touring revue to ruin his son's acting career.

With the coming of talkies came a reversal of roles: the actor now had to be heard and the camera had to be silenced. No longer free to roam at will, it was caged in a soundproof wooden booth, with a lead lining. This was mounted on an Austin 7 chassis with an optical glass window through which the film was shot, and 'action' was signalled through the glass to the deaf operator. This booth was to become known to the cameramen as a 'sweat box': as the sets heated up so did the unfortunate inmates, who would rush out for a breather or a hose-down when conditions became intolerable.

While the Musicians' Union was still demanding that only members should be employed in the rapidly dwindling cinema orchestras, due to the advent of sound, G.W. Emery (late Inland Revenue) was consoling readers of *The Spotlight Bulletin*, with the story of the indignant recipient of

It looks as if Betty Balfour has managed to *Raise the Roof* – with Maurice Evans (left), Ellis Jeffreys and Sam Livesey

Harvey Braban, seated between Anny Ondra and John Longden, in a scene of " Blackmail," with Alfred Hitchcock, the producer, standing by.

Mr. R. E. Jeffrey (standing), late B.B.C., sound production adviser, and Mr. J. A. Murray, superintending the sound recording in special chamber.

The camera man at work behind glass.

an Income Tax demand for two shillings and sixpence who had deducted sixpence from this horrendous sum for 'headache powders used as a result of studying the forms'. In the same weekly, eight-and-a-half-year-old Bunty was being advertised as '. . . very obedient . . . . has passed talkie test' – while Katie Johnson specialised in 'talking, sympathetic mother parts'. In 1929/30, it obviously paid off, to have passed your test.

Softly-spoken British actress Edna Best, once married to Herbert Marshall, starred next for John Maxwell in *Loose Ends* with Owen Nares, Adrienne Allen and Miles Mander; the film told the story of a lady reporter, blackmailed for her 'inside knowledge'. Best and Marshall teamed up in a number of films, but later in 1939, at the age of thirty-nine, she was to decide to try her luck in the American Hollywood.

B.I.P.'s 'First British Cineradio Revue', *Elstree Calling*, directed by Adrian Brunel and photographed by Claude Friese-Greene (son of a famous father), followed. It featured an impressive line-up

From the *Daily Mirror*, 11th April 1929

of film and radio stars of the day: Jack Hulbert, Cicely Courtneidge, Helen Burnell, Anna May Wong, Jameson Thomas, 'whose smile means rapture to the average flapper', Tommy Handley, Gordon Harker, the Charlot Girls, and many others. While some of the sketches may appear very unsophisticated by today's standards, to watch a young Tommy Handley at work, or Anna May Wong in a sendup of *The Taming of the Shrew*, is sheer delight. Some of the music came from the pen of a youthful composer called Ivor Novello.

Hitchcock had written much of the material for the light-hearted *Elstree Calling*, but his next film was *Murder* in which he devised 'the cinematic means of soliloquy' for his star, Herbert Marshall. Only Hitch perhaps could have conveyed with hands that resembled bunches of bananas, the delicacy of expression from inner thought for screen actors, rather than the facial overplay that had been required from silent stars.

ABOVE
Edna Best and Owen Nares in *Loose Ends*

LEFT
Warwick Ward as an Oriental Goldfinger with Dorothy
Seacombe in *The Yellow Mask*

BELOW
Lupino Lane, perhaps best remembered for his silent
comedies, enjoying a fantasy world in *The Yellow Mask*

A new confident John Maxwell put another
three films into production in the summer of 1930.
Young Woodley, with Madeleine Carroll, Sam
Livesey, Frank Lawton and Rene Ray; *Suspense*, a
war film, directed by D. Walter Summers; and *The
Yellow Mask*, a musical with Lupino Lane, Dorothy
Seacombe and Warwick Ward, about the robbery
of the crown jewels from the Tower of London, by a
Chinese type 'Goldfinger'.

The amazing J.D. Williams, the man who had
originally built the B.I.P. studios and gone back to
the States virtually penniless, was now back in the
British eye, as head of World Wide Pictures, U.S.A.
He put forward two major suggestions to the
British film industry: one was for the setting up of a
twenty-stage, multi-national studio in the Elstree
district; the other for the setting up of a 'British
Motion Picture Academy' with the double object of
stimulating experimental production and training
new talent.

Monty Banks was now to direct *The Black Hand
Gang* with Wee Georgie Wood playing the chief of a
children's gang, who set out to thwart a burglary.
Monty's Italian temperament was exceeded only
by that of his wife Gladys Frazin, an ample
American actress who always looked as if a
diamond chandelier had recently descended on
her. Their stormy domestic scenario far outdid

BERNARD SHAW the Famous Dramatist, and JOHN MAXWELL Chairman of the British International Pictures Ltd.,
showing the former signing the contract for the talkie version of his play
"HOW HE LIED TO HER HUSBAND."

anything that was taking place on set and the technicians would await with anticipation and betting slips the condition of the battered husband, complete with black eye or bandaged head. Tragically Miss Frazin was eventually to commit suicide and in time Gracie Fields was to become the second Mrs Banks.

While comedian Leslie Fuller, who was to star in a number of B.I.P. comedies, was making *Not so quiet on the Western Front*, rumour was afoot that George Bernard Shaw had agreed to let one of the founder forces of the B.B.C., Cecil Lewis, make a talkie of *How He Lied to her Husband*. On two conditions: that Lewis should direct the film, and that the play should be filmed uncut and without alterations to the script. Without fuss Maxwell agreed and a seventy-four-year-old, eagle-eyed

LEFT
Edmund Gwenn, Vera Lennox and Robert Harris in Shaw's *How He Lied to her Husband*

RIGHT
Laurence Olivier and Nora Swinburne in *Potiphar's Wife*

Sam Livesey, as Mr Simmons, with an attentive audience in *Young Woodley*

Shaw was constantly on set to instruct film beginner Edmund Gwenn as the husband/lover, Vera Lennox and Robert Harris in the finer points of their business. Although it did not enhance the Elstree coffers – filmed as if from the theatre stalls – it was a brave attempt by B.I.P. into the unknown.

As 1930 drew to a close John Maxwell splurged into a flurry of four productions. *Cape Forlorn* with Fay Compton and Ian Hunter was followed by *Potiphar's Wife*, in which an actor with a riveting voice and face played a minor role. His new actress bride Jill Esmond, seemed to be happily torn between her two new roles: that of the heroine of *The Chinese Bungalow*, being made across the road, and that of Mrs Laurence Olivier. *The Middle Watch*, directed by Norman Walker, with Owen Nares and Dodo Watts, was a naval comedy in which the heroine stows away to the discomfiture of her officer fiance; and *Uneasy Virtue* with Francis Lister and Edmund Breon, also included newcomer Molly Lamont from South Africa, who was to become a firm favourite with British audiences.

By the end of 1930, it was clear that sound had won the day and that it was all over bar the Silents shouting.

Although he had achieved a strong head start and a startling four 'firsts' for B.I.P. Elstree, John Maxwell was going to have to look to his laurels. The British and Dominions Studios, Blattner Studios and Gate Studios at Elstree were hot on his heels and he knew it. But the lead had been established – and the game afoot now was to try to hold on to it.

Chapter 4
The Golden Thirties

IF the thirties had started off badly for the industry as a whole, B.I.P. surged ahead with the confidence of the early initiator. It was during these years that the 'British Hollywood' was firmly established.

With a lead not only in sound features but also a remarkable library of shorts to their credit, they commenced production of *Keepers of Youth* which gave Ann Todd one of her first major film roles and was directed by Thomas Bentley, by now well-established at Elstree. A unique dress sense apart, he would prepare a quaint card index system for camera moves and would be furious at any script changes, while his cast were driven to distraction by his incomparable 'acting aids'. The first was that after he had shouted 'Action' the actors should silently count up to four before delivery. Clearly a case for E.S.P. The second was in the shape of an eccentric type of music stand, on which he insisted they concentrate during action to assist camera line-up; thus ensuring a cross-eyed appearance, after prolonged concentration and limited movement and technique. Nevertheless the film, which centred around Garry Marsh as the new games master playing with the affections of Ann Todd, the matron of a public school, was well received and had an excellent Launder script.

Certainly actors were required to be something more than flexible at this time. *The Flying Fool*, a stage success, directed by Walter Summers and photographed by Claude Friese-Greene, starred Benita Hume, Ursula Jeans and Henry Kendall.

Kendall had landed the role in the face of stiff opposition from some of the Elstree executives who argued that he was not a star name. Considering that they had Leslie Howard in mind for the part, this was not surprising. But perhaps even Kendall had not realised just how versatile he was going to have to be. The story line concerned a secret service pilot who is helped by a crook's moll and, in the course of the action, is drugged and thrown into a sewer. On stage this had all been fine: the flying bit had, not unnaturally, been taken for granted, while the sewer effect had been created by a transparent tank draped with brown gauze aided by some murky green 'spots'. Understandably 'Captain' Summers, the director, did not visualise his film in these stage terms. He built a huge tank

BELOW
Two Worlds, produced by E. A. Dupont in 1930 for B.I.P., with Norah Baring and Randle Ayrton

The Flying Fool was Henry Kendall, seen here with Benita Hume

in B.I.P.'s largest studio and prepared for a three-day shoot. In freezing water, Kendall was called upon to dive under a grille in plus-fours. Each time he made the attempt the plus-fours would fill up like an enormous pair of water wings – and the fact that he was covered in lard, against the cold, hindered rather than helped the situation – but this was just a warm-up.

The next stunt required Kendall to pursue a Handley-Page aircraft along a tarmac and jump into it on take-off. He was also required to fly *and* photograph at the same time, which he did. Not surprisingly he finished up in hospital with blood poisoning – studio terminology for exhaustion – but the film was a tremendous box-office success.

Rather more attractive water was to be provided for former music-hall artist, Ernie Lotinga in *Josser Joins the Navy*. The Josser comedies – *P.C. Josser*, *Josser in the Army* and so on – were to become cult films of their time, with a tremendous following.

Directing *Josser Joins the Navy* was Norman Lee,

'Oh, Grandma, what big eyes you've got!' Renee Gadd with Grandma (Ernie Lotinga) in *Josser Joins the Navy*

who had secured that position with a certain cunning. Prior to the film, his career had reached an all-time low and he was grateful to receive commissions for film articles to various magazines under the nom de plume of Miss X. Miss X was to write that she had seen Mr Lee watching Alfred Hitchcock direct at Elstree and went on: 'Why do film studios neglect this up-and-coming producer? Instead of standing idly by watching other people direct films, Lee should be doing the job himself.'

A month later, Walter Mycroft, head of production for John Maxwell, signed up Mr Lee.

Whether it was a necessary release from the authoritarian approach of the Elstree bosses, or the fact that the young industry in the thirties was beginning to sparkle in its own right with its own stars and personalities – or perhaps a fatal blend of both – is a matter for speculation. The fact remains, however, that while 'The Old Man' (John Maxwell) or his two right hands, young Robert Clark and Walter Mycroft were about, a stern business-like

Comedian Leslie Fuller in *Poor Old Bill*

atmosphere pervaded the studio. But the moment their backs were turned directors, stars and staff alike would embark on a series of schoolboy practical jokes and pranks which were to make a combination of *The Boys Own*, *The Beano* and Fatty Arbuckle appear like *The Pilgrim's Progress*.

Alfred Hitchcock, Monty Banks, Sonnie Hale, Bobby Howes and Cliff Mollison were the chief offenders.

It started with 'fly-ripping' (ripping open fly buttons) while the victim was engaged in carrying props or swinging a sound boom, and went on to such items as 'windmill-blowing wagers' which would leave the unsuspecting winner to saunter around the studios with lamp-blackened face. The leading exponent was Hitchcock who had a kind of court jester in the shape of prop man Harry Thorn. Hitch gravely explained that it would be much appreciated if Harry would manipulate some clock hands to strike the hour – quite normal except that the clock was above the mantelpiece, over a fireplace and Harry had to scramble up the chimney to perform the task. Before calling 'Shoot',

Hitch whispered for the fire to be lit, and a coughing, blackened Harry could be seem scrambling over the set top. To alleviate boredom Hitchcock would take to lighting fires under chairs, in which recumbent actors passed the time, or have someone's new car gaily striped, in washable paint.

Terrified that word of these happenings would filter through to Maxwell, the studio manager, the now legendary Joe Grossman, called the ringleaders together and stuttered that it all had to stop. Shamefaced and with bowed heads they agreed – then ripped his flies open. In this case

RIGHT
Glamour, made for B.I.P. in 1931, starred Seymour Hicks, Ellaline Terris and a young Beverley Nichols

BELOW
Hitchcock's *Rich and Strange* may not have been an outstanding success, but its stars, Henry Kendall, Percy Marmont (standing), Joan Barry and Betty Amann continued to be great favourites at the box office

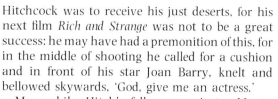

Hitchcock was to receive his just deserts, for his next film *Rich and Strange* was not to be a great success: he may have had a premonition of this, for in the middle of shooting he called for a cushion and in front of his star Joan Barry, knelt and bellowed skywards, 'God, give me an actress.'

Meanwhile, Hitch's fellow conspirator Monty Banks had directed a low budget movie *My Wife's Family* with Clapham-born heart-throb Gene Gerrard and Molly Lamont and while it received the boot from the press, it did very well at the box office. Banks was to make two more comedies for Maxwell in 1931: *Money for Nothing* starring Seymour Hicks, Edmund Gwenn and Donald Calthrop, the story of a gambler mistaken for a financier; and *Tonight's the Night* with Leslie Fuller, in which singer Betty Fields, younger sister of Gracie, had a tiny part.

'Quota quickies' or not, John Maxwell seemed to throw his customary caution to the wind in favour of his many box offices in the thirties, with all the star names that he could muster or inveigle from Britain or the U.S.A. Lupino Lane directed *The Love Race* for him, along with *Love Lies*, starring his cousin Stanley Lupino and Binnie Barnes, while Malcolm Sargent conducted the New Symphony Orchestra in B.I.P.'s *Gypsy Blood*.

Yes, Mr Maxwell was even prepared to take a gamble with a musical comedy star called Jessie Matthews. But the new Mrs Sonnie Hale was to be less than enchanted with her first major movie. Life in the theatre had not disciplined her to a 6 a.m. call or performing within narrow chalk lines so as to remain in focus. Gene Gerrard was to direct as well as star in *Out Of The Blue* with Jessie and, popular though he was with his audience, he had had virtually no experience as a director. It was also regretfully concluded by the cameramen, that Matthews was far from photogenic. She came away from Elstree convinced that she was the freak of the century and would never make another film, little realising that within a year she was to be hailed as Britain's brightest film discovery.

On the set of *My Wife's Family*, Clapham-born heart-throb Gene Gerrard, Muriel Angelus, director Monty Banks (in wheelchair) and, far right, leaning nonchalantly against his famous camera's 'sweat box' is Claude Friese-Greene, son of William Friese-Greene, inventor of one of the first practical cinematograph cameras. Standing behind Monty Banks is a young Mario Zampi

Out of the Blue with the new Mrs Sonnie Hale, Jessie Matthews (left) and Kay Hammond

Smash hit *Goodnight Vienna* with Anna Neagle (seated) and Jack Buchanan having problems with the telephone. On one occasion, Herbert Wilcox revived his exhausted cast with real champagne, producing sparkling results

The Jessie Matthews/Sonnie Hale romance probably triggered off an opportunity for a young actress for whom Matthews had the highest admiration. Her name was Anna Neagle. Jessie Matthews and the inimitable Jack Buchanan had been stage partners but parted after a tiff. Young Anna was then offered a part in *Stand Up and Sing* by Buchanan, which she accepted.

The show was a great success and during the run, film producer Herbert Wilcox (who had leased studios from John Maxwell at B.I.P. and started his own British and Dominions Film Corporation) strolled into the London Hippodrome and stood at the back of the stalls. He took one look at the lovely Miss Neagle and decided that she was ideal for a role he had been trying to cast in his next film *Goodnight Vienna* – their partnership was to last for forty-six years.

With the studio back-to-back arrangement between B.I.P. and British Dominions, there was great camaraderie between stars and staff, who watched each other at work and used the B.I.P. restaurant. This, in addition to the presence of the Blattner and Whitehall studios, both within five minutes of the Maxwell complex, certainly paved

the way for the 'British Hollywood' tag that was to last throughout the thirties.

If Maxwell was the businessman of the industry, then Wilcox was certainly the showman. The British and Dominions Studios were the first in Europe to be equipped with sound by Western Electric. By 1931, Wilcox had already made a number of films at Elstree; encouraged Michael Balcon to hire B. and D. to make two Leslie Henson sound comedies; made two Aldwych Farces, photographic versions of the stage plays *Rookery Nook* and *The Chance of a Night Time*, with Tom Walls and Ralph Lynn; and signed up Jack Buchanan and a cameraman by the name of Freddie Young, who was to win international acclaim and three Oscars. Despite her inexperience, Anna Neagle's dedication, matched with a subtle charm and freshness, melted into the professionalism and hearts of these three established film makers, Wilcox, Buchanan and Young and she became part of their team. While always retaining her interest in the theatre, she went on to become one of our greatest film stars and made many films at Elstree including *Goodnight Vienna*, *The Flag Lieutenant*, *The Little Damozel* and *Nell Gwyn*.

Back on the B.I.P. lot the now established Norman Lee was creating something of a sensation by insisting on draping, without draping, three lovely nudes on his set of *Strip, Strip, Hooray*. The girls were paid three guineas a day and the set was cleared except for essential workers, surprising even Lee as to the number of staff who thought their contribution indispensable. Joe Grossman's nervous twitch took on new dimensions as he surveyed the scene, imagined the 'Old Man's' apoplexy and gave a strangled 'Blimey, nude dames!' Not much escaped John Maxwell however. Schoolboy pranks were one thing, moral issues quite another, and a quiet word was passed down to Walter Mycroft to get the matter covered up, in more ways than one. It could be that Mr Mycroft was not one hundred per cent successful. Every decade produces its own critic on public morality and the thirties produced the Hon. Mrs Eleanor Plumer, who attacked the British film industry on the grounds that they relied too much on '. . . bathroom scenes, wrong bedroom entanglements, mothers-in-law and an endless display of legs and undergarments' – in that order. By comparison, school children of that period seemed to have a distinctly more mature list of priorities for improve-

One of the famous Aldwych farces so popular in the early thirties – *Rookery Nook*, with (left to right) Ethel Coleridge, Ralph Lynn, Tom Walls, Winifred Shotter and Robertson Hare

John Stuart, Anne Grey and Donald Calthrop in *Number Seventeen*, the story of the reformation of a lady jewel thief who assists a detective to foil a gang's getaway

ments in film entertainment. 'No smoking, no babies and the front seats moved to the back.'

But even the Hon. Mrs Plumer could not have taken exception to *Number Seventeen* with Anne Gray and Barry Jones, with director Hitchcock using the Schufftan Process for certain shots. This was a means of combining life-size action with models, achieved by angles, reflected lights and images. But a month later Gray and Jones were themselves to become critical of the love/hate relationship that existed between B.I.P. and George Bernard Shaw. Both were to star in *Arms and the Man* and in their wisdom the studios were once again to assure Shaw that he would have complete scenario control and that his theatrical script

Gene Gerrard, former beauty queen Molly Lamont and
practical joker director Monty Banks in *Leave It To Me*

would remain untouched – for good measure they
then added that they would shoot in North Wales,
not perhaps the best of places for stilted theatrical
dialogue accompanied by the technical limitations
of the day. The film was to lose the studio a lot of
money and terminate the well-intentioned but
fateful association of B.I.P. and G.B.S.

On a more cheerful note the irresistible Gertie
Lawrence was to star in Hitchcock's production of
Lord Camber's Ladies, the men in her life at that time
being Sir Gerald du Maurier her leading man and
the film's director Benn Levy, an impossible situation for anyone but Gertie. Lawrence and du
Maurier were both people of the theatre and both
at that period in worrying financial situations.
While applying themselves professionally to the
comedy/thriller about a lord trying to poison his
actress wife in order to marry a nurse (Benita
Hume) their safety valves appeared in a series of
bizarre and juvenile jokes. Aided and abetted by
the cherub-faced Hitchcock, they plunged the

studios once again into a frenzy of jumping
crackers and bogus messages, accompanied by a
haggard Joe Grossman. Two months later, after a
series of lectures, pleading and eventually threats
from the management, two of the jokers, Monty
Banks and Bobby Howes, went into production of
For Love of Mike in docile fashion; all was quiet on
the studio front – for the time being.

By mid-1933 the Associated British Picture
Corporation (A.B.P.C.) had been formed by John
Maxwell as the holding company to take over the
capital of B.I.P., B.I.F., Wardour Films, Pathe
Pictures, and his original A.B.C. circuit of 147
cinemas, but the studios were still to be known as
B.I.P. until 1939. B.I.P. and B. and D. at Elstree still
had the field very much to themselves locally. The

RIGHT
He may have a good bedside manner, but in fact
Gerald du Maurier is planning the demise of his actress
wife (Gertrude Lawrence) in *Lord Camber's Ladies*

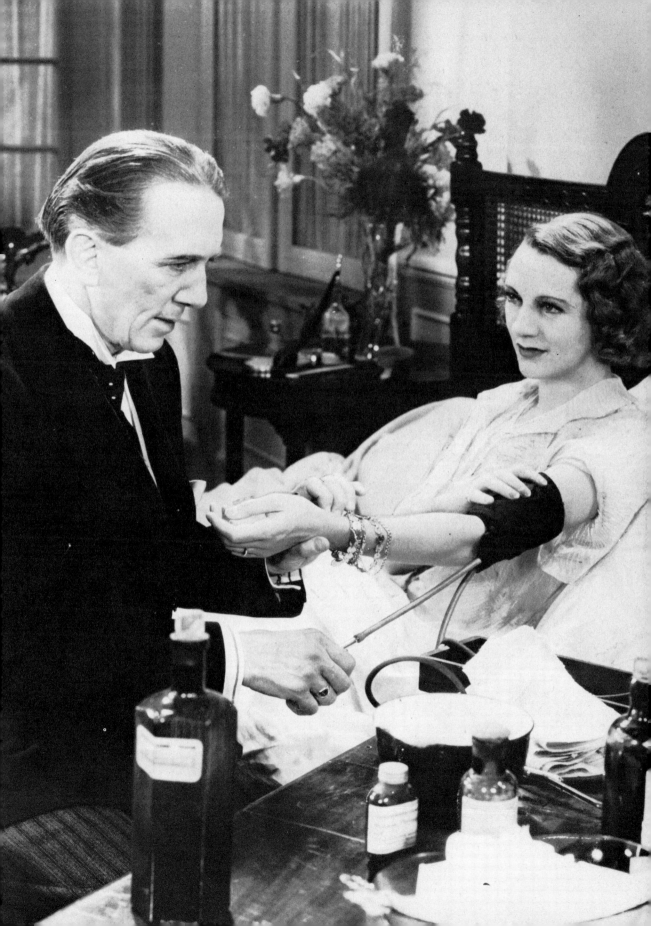

TOP
Raquel Torres in *Red Wagon*

ABOVE
Charles Bickford in *Red Wagon*

Paul Stein, Richard Eichberg, Marcel Varnel, Otto Kanturek, and Paul Merzbach were all to work at B.I.P. over the next few years and in a number of cases they were helped personally by Maxwell. Robert Clark was later to tell a story, against himself, of one of them asking for financial production assistance, without any collateral except his wife's jewellery. An enthusiastic young Clark accepted and was in turn verbally flayed by an outraged Maxwell, who insisted that the jewels be returned with a personal offer of help.

One of this number, Paul Stein, directed *Red Wagon* in 1933 for B.I.P. It was a successful, expensive film starring American actress Raquel Torres, Charles Bickford and Greta Nissen; other credits included Leslie Norman as film editor and child actor Jimmy Hanley.

The arrival of Miss Torres had created quite a stir and Maxwell continued to invite American stars to his British Hollywood, including Buddy Rogers, Ben Lyon and Bebe Daniels. Ben was to make *I Spy*, a comedy about a playboy mistaken for a Ruritanian spy, with Sally Eilers; and Bebe was to star in *A Southern Maid* with Clifford Mollison and Lupino Lane. She was to become a firm favourite at the studio and Elstree residents were by this time becoming quite blasé about seeing both British and American stars in their midst. Certainly many of the stars and producers were beginning to take up residence in and around Elstree, expanding the Hollywood image still further, while elegant residential clubs such as the Aldenham House Club, Elstree Country Club and Radnor Hall, whose visitors' books would have delighted autograph hunters then and now, mushroomed into glamorous luxury.

Wilcox, too, was pressing ahead with his American and European contacts. In 1933 he leased one of his British and Dominion sound stages to Paramount British on a ten-year lease and Alexander Korda found himself making *The Private Life of Henry VIII* on a B. and D. stage after a distribution snag in which Wilcox had an exclusive contract with United Artists. The astute Wilcox made an exception for Korda on the condition that his film was made at the B. and D.

Visiting the Elstree set, actress Maria Corda had drawn her husband's attention to a petite, striking brunette with a hint of Asian beauty about her. He appeared non-committal but in fact directed the girl's test himself and she was offered the tiny part of Anne Boleyn in his film. Her name was Merle

Blattner studios had just gone bankrupt, although they were to be reborn again very shortly, and the Whitehall's fortunes came and went.

For a 'man without a heart', as he was called by some outsiders, Maxwell was to demonstrate imaginative and humane traits that were to leave even his sternest critics silenced, by welcoming to Elstree a number of continental producers and directors, who for political and religious reasons were beginning to experience difficult times within their own countries in the thirties.

RIGHT
Caught in the act! Poor Ben Lyon is apprehended by
monocled Dennis Hoey and Henry Victor. H. F. Maltby
looks on authoritatively from his splendid seat of
power in *I Spy*

BELOW
Bebe Daniels, who was to have a long and happy
married and professional partnership with Ben Lyon,
pictured here with handsome star Clifford Mollison in
A Southern Maid

Heads We Go, a B.I.P. comedy about a model who poses as a filmstar's double, starring (left to right) Binnie Barnes, Constance Cummings, Gus McNaughton and Claude Hulbert

BELOW
Ralph Richardson and Ann Todd seen here with director Walter Summers on the set of *The Return of Bulldog Drummond*, made at B.I.P.'s Elstree and Welwyn studios

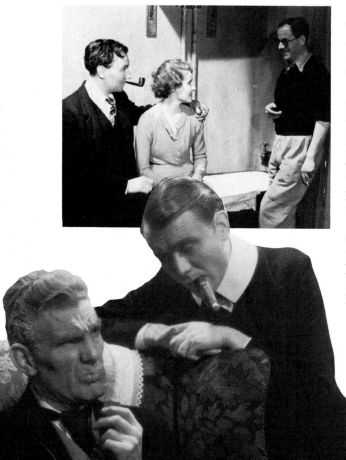

Oberon. She was to become a star and, in due course, Mrs Alexander Korda. *The Private Life of Henry VIII* starred Charles Laughton and Robert Donat; it was an outstanding success and opened many hitherto locked distribution and funding doors abroad – comparable to the kind of success that *Chariots of Fire* was to achieve for Britain nearly fifty years later.

As well as his dealings with Korda and Paramount British, and his ongoing successes with Anna Neagle, Wilcox had by this time made Freddie Young head of photography and was surging ahead with his partnership with Jack Buchanan. Between 1933 and 1936, with the success of *Goodnight Vienna* still ringing in their ears, he made five musicals with Buchanan, including *Yes Mr Brown* and *Brewster's Millions*. As a result, Jack, the adored matinee idol and film star, realised just how much his own personal publicity could add to a film's success. He became progressively more involved in their films' distribution and became a truly professional 'tub-thumper'.

Meantime John Maxwell was making *Those were the Days* adapted from Sir Arthur Pinero's play *The Magistrate*. It starred Will Hay in his feature debut, Angela Baddeley and John Mills as the magistrate's twenty-one-year-old stepson.

Director Thomas Bentley once again brought his unique talents to the production. Hay had been a little reluctant to commence a film career; he was, after all, earning £800 per week as a variety star, so Bentley (a one time music-hall artist himself) decided to intersperse the story with a series of variety acts, that would appeal to both Hay and his public. He succeeded and Will Hay's film future was assured.

While Ralph Richardson and Ann Todd were making *Return of Bulldog Drummond* for B.I.P. at this time, three of Maxwell's continental directors, Paul Merzbach, Marcel Varnel and Paul Stein, were each preparing a new presentation. Merzbach's new comedy *Love at Second Sight* was to include Claude Hulbert and Stanley Holloway in its cast, while the Varnel film starred Clifford Mollison and Wendy Barrie as the romantic leads in *Freedom of the Seas*, but it was Paul Stein who was to direct B.I.P.'s blockbuster of the thirties.

LEFT
Those were the Days, adapted from Sir Arthur Pinero's play *The Magistrate*. It starred Will Hay as the Magistrate and John Mills as his stepson

Blossom Time was the Sound of Music of its day and an outstanding success. Artistically ahead of its time in terms of sets and costumes, it starred Richard Tauber and Jane Baxter and it was shot by Otto Kanturek and Bryan Langley. Set in Vienna in 1826, it told of a composer's love for a girl, who is, of course, in love with someone else. An important sound development was made when Tauber sang live to the accompaniment of a London choir – a fairly normal event, except that the choir was being relayed over the telephone then broadcast as a background to Tauber. Although adored by his public Tauber was inclined to be temperamental and Stein in turn became edgy. He exploded with anger when he saw that four white horses that he had expressly ordered for the film were in fact dappled. Feeling that a certain imaginative flair was called for, Robert Lennard (later to be head of casting) and the crew coaxed the handlers over to the pub and proceeded to spray the dapples with whitewash. Thinking that new horses had been obtained Stein was delighted, until the paint began to crack and flutter like snow flakes under the arc lights.

In the mid-thirties a rustle of Elstree leaves was really signifying the beginning of the wind of change, not only for the British Hollywood, but also for the British film industry. The Blattner Studios were undergoing changes and would

OVERLEAF
The Blossom Time set: an important sound development was made when Richard Tauber sang live to the accompaniment of a London choir – a fairly normal event, except that the choir was being relayed over the telephone, then broadcast as a background to Tauber's scene

BELOW
Lovely Tamara Desni played the heroine in McGlusky the Sea Rover, made in 1935. Professional boxer Jack Doyle, cast as McGlusky, becomes involved with a gang of gun-runners and falls in love with an Arab girl

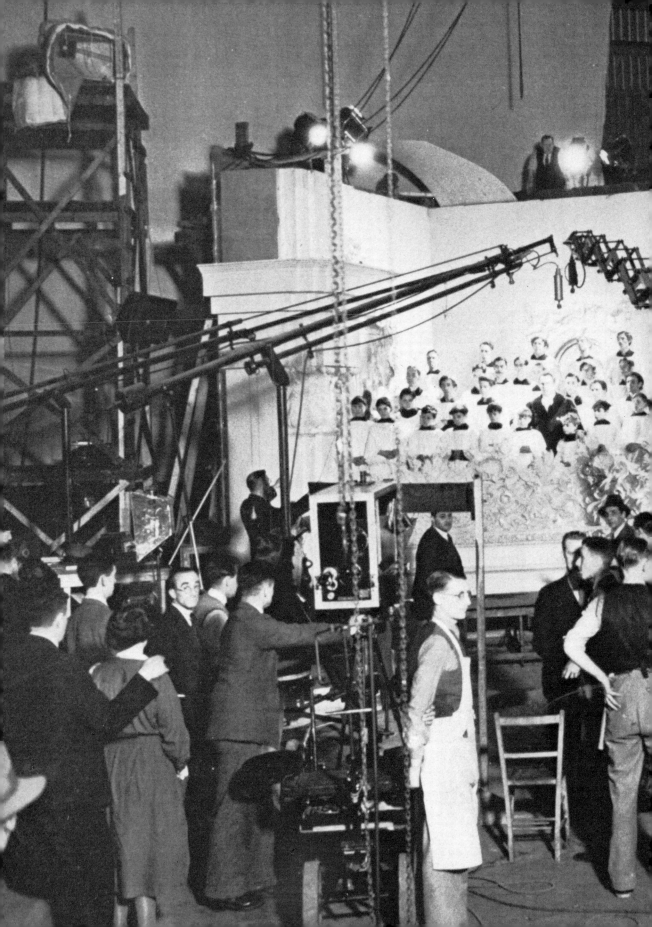

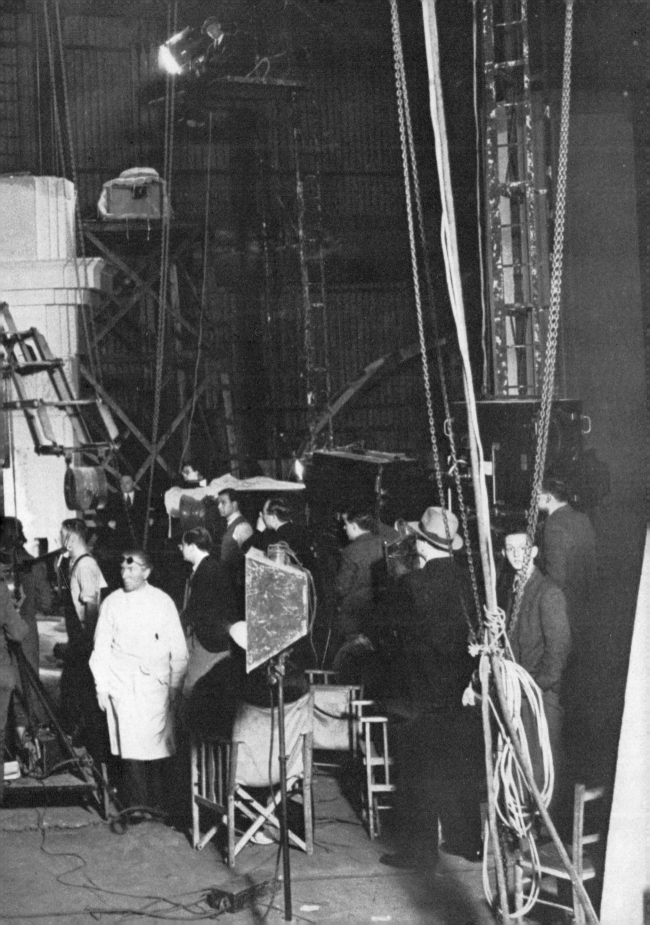

become the Rock Studios, owned by Joe Rock. They would in turn be bought in the early forties by Lady Yule, widow of a jute millionaire, and renamed the British National Studios. A brilliant businessman by the name of J. Arthur Rank, who was new to the industry in the thirties, had made a film with her company in 1935 called *The Turn of the Tide*; although he had only entered the industry to make religious films or stories with a strong moral fibre he was appalled to find that he was unable to obtain a release on the Gaumont circuit for his film, which led him to gain control over his own production and distribution – and thus the J.

BELOW
Adrienne Ames and Nils Asther in *Abdul the Damned*

ABOVE
Abdul the Damned, also made in 1935, had some of the most spectacular sets and costumes (by B. J. Simmons and Bermans) of the time. It also starred four of the leading names of the day: Fritz Kortner and Adrienne Ames (seen here), Nils Asther and John Stuart

RIGHT
Adrienne Ames in *Abdul the Damned*

JUNE CLYDE
BUDDY ROGERS

FRED EMNEY

OLIVER WAKEFIELD
ZELMA O'NEAL
LAWRENCE ANDERSON
IRIS HOEY
CLAUD ALLISTER

HARRY ACRES
LEADER OF THE MASSED

CLAIRE LUCE

Produced by Walter Mycroft for A.B.P.C., *Let's Make a Night of It* starred American leading man Buddy Rogers and featured many popular dance bands of the period

Mary Pickford on the set of *Let's Make a Night of It*, visiting Buddy Rogers, whom she married after her divorce from Douglas Fairbanks Senior

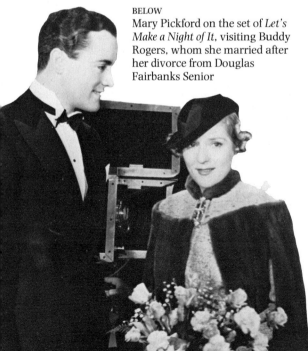

Arthur Rank Film Organisation came into being.

Down the road, Julius Hagen was planning his new studios at the old Whitehall Studios and rumours were afoot that the Soskin family were going to build an ultra-modern film studio that would knock even an American Hollywood complex into a 'cocked hat'.

But in the lull before the storm it was business as usual at the B.I.P. and B. and D. studios. True, there had been a strike during the making of *Blossom Time*, but it had all been very much a family affair with John Maxwell still firmly in charge, no other studios involved and a happy settlement for all concerned of an extra penny halfpenny per hour. Who could be upset after all, when the studio was making such films as *Mimi*, the film version of *La Bohème* with Douglas Fairbanks Junior and Gertrude Lawrence.

Delicious, unchanged and unrepentant as ever, Miss Lawrence was still involved with her leading man, still deeply in debt and still up to her old mischievous pranks on set. Equally unrepentant and equally unchanged, naughty Monty Banks

was once again getting up to his old tricks on the *Dandy Dick* set.

Dandy Dick was another Pinero adaptation, and Will Hay was once again to star, in a story about a vicar unjustly suspected of horse doping and arson. Hay was terrified of horses and became chalk-faced with fear every time he had to approach one during a scene, particularly as the docile beast seemed to become especially frisky the moment he got within sugar-giving distance. He did not know until later that Monty Banks was lying on his stomach behind the wicker set, tickling the horse's private parts with a long straw. But stardom, even in the thirties, had its rewards: for *Dandy Dick* Hay was paid in the region of £1,500 for five weeks work, while supporting actors Kathleen Harrison and Moore Marriott, were paid about eight pounds per day for a much shorter period.

Royalty followed, in the shape of a Queen, a King and a Princess. Athene Seyler played Elizabeth I in *Drake of England* with Matheson Lang as Drake. The film co-starred Jane Baxter, Henry Mollison and Donald Wolfit, with Ronald Neame and Jack Parker on camera. The King was George V, in

Athene Seyler as Queen Elizabeth in *Drake of England*

Will Hay and Nancy Burne in *Dandy Dick*, the story of a vicar unjustly suspected of horse doping and arson

LEFT
Diana Napier and Douglas Fairbanks Junior in *Mimi*, the film version of *La Bohème*

Matinee idol of the twenties Matheson Lang in *Drake of England*, a B.I.P. production of 1935

Ivan Samson (left) as the Grand Duke, Grete Natzler as the Princess Helene (a Spurs supporter?) and Patric Knowles as Max Brandt in *The Student's Romance*

LEFT
British Lilian Harvey, who became a top star in Germany, with Carl Esmond in *Invitation to the Waltz*

BELOW
Richard Tauber and Diana Napier met and married while filming at Elstree. A close encounter from *Heart's Desire*

whose honour and to mark whose jubilee *Royal Cavalcade*, a history from 1910–1935, was made; while the Princess was played by Grete Natzler in *The Student's Romance* – a sort of *Student Prince* in reverse, when the commoner student, played by Patric Knowles, falls in love with a princess, posing as a poor subject. Some early fencing scenes had been dubbed by a young man who was at that time busy commuting between the Northampton Repertory Company and Teddington studios. On a visit to Elstree, Jack Warner saw the rushes and, having already been advised by Irving Asher, head of Teddington, to sign him up, did just that. The result was that Errol Flynn went to the States, made *Captain Blood* and became an international star.

Four musicals were to bounce B.I.P. into 1936. *I Give My Heart*, from the operetta *The Dubarry*, with Gitta Alpar and Owen Nares; *Invitation to the Waltz*, whose ballet scenes were devised and danced by Anton Dolin, with Clarence Elder in charge of art direction; *Heart's Desire*, another Viennese and indeed Elstree romance, starring Richard Tauber and Diana Napier, who had met and married while filming at B.I.P., and the ever popular Henry Hall with his B.B.C. Dance Orchestra in *Music Hath Charms*. The proposed film credits were also to note '. . . by courtesy of the Columbia Graphophone Company' and suggest 'Fairly – but not *too* small'!

The fragmented and complex nature of the modern British film industry is due in a large part to the complicated developments that took place from 1936 onwards, not only as a result of various acts of governmental support or non-support, depending on the party of the day, but also due to the power struggles that existed within the industry at that time, between the major British film consortiums and their battles for production, distribution and exhibition supremacy.

John Maxwell had always kept a low public profile; not for him the showmanship at which Wilcox and others excelled. The 'Old Man', as he

Henry Hall with his B.B.C. Dance Orchestra in *Music Hath Charms*

was known affectionately, presented a stern but just image to his staff. He was never seen without a hat and never, but never – good Scot as he was – with either money or matches in his pocket. His private life was to remain just that, from start to finish. It came as something of a surprise then to perhaps himself and the industry, to see his fierce and public involvement in an inter-company punch-up in 1936. Gaumont-British, his major rival, had floundered into an outsize overdraft and Maxwell, with a keen take-over bid in hand, announced to the press that it had been successful and that henceforth he would head both Gaumont and Associated British (B.I.P.).

In fact this was not to happen. Twentieth Century Fox had long owned a portion of the Gaumont gateaux and while Maxwell negotiated in London with the board from Gaumont, Isidore Ostrer, fearful of the inevitable monopoly if five to six hundred cinemas fell into one pair of hands, negotiated in New York with the president of Twentieth Century Fox. The outcome was a deal that did not include Maxwell. The rules of this new ball game were not to Maxwell's liking. Astounded and disappointed he sued the Ostrer group over the share sales and lost, then quietly went out and bought another 130 cinemas. In the background J. Arthur Rank, who even in this short space of time had built his own Pinewood Studios, watched and waited.

But a catastrophe of far greater dimensions happened to Elstree in 1936. In the early hours of a

frosty February morning, fire had swept through the British and Dominion Studios, belonging to Herbert Wilcox, leaving a smoking gutted wreckage. Only the valiant work of the local fire brigade, headed by Joe Grossman and many of the staff, prevented the fire from spreading into the B.I.P. studios, literally yards away. Wilcox and Maxwell were stunned, but with a resilience unique to the industry, Wilcox took his courage and insurance money in both hands and looked for new premises.

Although desperately anxious for help, Maxwell was not in a position to offer Wilcox the necessary backing and facilities a second time around, but someone else was and Herbert Wilcox started afresh at the new Pinewood Studios.

Elstree as a whole was badly shaken at the demise of the B. and D. studios. Studio workers, hotels and shops were dismayed to find that half of their earning potential had been lost literally overnight. But – typical of show business – two stories emerged to lighten the gloom. The first was

ABOVE
Some form of explanation seems necessary from Robertson Hare (in drag), but bald Alfred Drayton and rose-clutching Billy Milton seem far from convinced in *Aren't Men Beasts*, a 1937 B.I.P. comedy

Another heart-throb of the thirties, John Lodge, seen here with Dorothy Mackaill in *Bulldog Drummond At Bay*

that Wilcox had given a generous handout to a weary fireman with instructions to buy a crate of whisky for the officers and ten crates of beer for the men, but both the quantities and status had been reversed. The other concerned the notepaper of Irish director Herbert Brenon, who obviously felt that he should hedge his bets. It was headed 'Home Farm, Elstree' and added, 'New laid eggs and table poultry for sale'. Still, Mr Brenon need not have had too many sleepless nights. A little later he was to direct *Someone at the Door* for John Maxwell, though his star Aileen Marson experienced something of a nightmare during the filming. Tied to a chair for a tense scene she was to experience instant withdrawal symptoms at first hand when a shout went up that a lion had escaped on an adjoining set. An expendable 'props' was lowered to cut her bonds and whisk her to safety.

***

Intent on supplying product to his now vast cinema chain, Maxwell had always been happy to lease part of his studios to independent producers,

Tied to a chair for a tense scene in *Someone at the Door*, Aileen Marson experienced instant withdrawal symptoms at first hand when a shout went up that a lion had escaped from an adjoining set. We assume that Billy Milton also managed to escape

as well as keeping his own production in full swing. In 1937 and 1938, with Walter Mycroft still as head of production he continued to make films at an incredible rate. They were to include Edgar Wallace's *The Terror* with Wilfred Lawson, Bernard Lee and Alastair Sim: *Housemaster*, a comedy about a schoolboy rebellion against the new headmaster's reforms, which starred Diana Churchill, Rene Ray and Cecil Parker; *Star of the Circus* with Otto Kruger, John Clements and Patrick Barr; and *Yellow Sands* with Dame Marie Tempest, Coral Browne and a lovable rascal of a man whose special star quality was to be sadly submerged by the tide of the star quality liquid that he consumed, Robert Newton.

But it was perhaps Maxwell's courageous and imaginative backing of Erich Pommer's Mayflower Picture Corporation, that really caught the public

ABOVE

Evensong line-up from *Housemaster*, including Diana Churchill (second from left), Rene Ray, Otto Kruger and Cecil Parker

RIGHT

Vivien Leigh and Rex Harrison in *St Martin's Lane*, another Erich Pommer film from the Mayflower Picture Corporation

BELOW

If looks could kill, Elsa Lanchester would certainly be on borrowed time, seen here with Charles Laughton in one of Erich Pommer's productions, *Vessel of Wrath*, based on a short story by W. Somerset Maugham. Laughton was to star in all three Pommer films made at Elstree in the late thirties and bring his inimitable skills to bear on each contrasting role

eye in the late thirties. With Charles Laughton in each production, Pommer was to make three films of quality with star performances. Based on a Somerset Maugham story, *Vessel of Wrath* co-starred Elsa Lanchester and Robert Newton and told of a drunken beachcomber who is reformed by a missionary's sister; *St Martin's Lane*, a Cockney romance, starred Vivien Leigh and Rex Harrison; while lovely Maureen O'Hara appeared in *Jamaica Inn* with Leslie Banks.

With world attention focusing on Europe and the threatening presence of World War Two, John Maxwell may well have pondered on the future of his own film empire early in 1939. But in order to prosper one still had to expand and to this end he

ABOVE
Jamaica Inn lobby card

ABOVE RIGHT
Postman Wilfrid Hyde-White is not the happiest of men in *Poison Pen*. He is seen here with Marjorie Rhodes and Edward Chapman, whilst Edward Rigby stares suspiciously at Flora Robson

RIGHT
Still wet behind the ears, Diana Churchill looks on with some concern as Bobby Howes gets a going over from Bertha Belmore and Wylie Watson in *Yes Madam*, an A.B.P.C. musical of 1938

The Gang's All Here lobby card: from left to right, Jack Buchanan, Googie Withers, Edward Everett Horton and Jack la Rue

cast a speculative eye over the brand new Amalgamated Studios at Elstree. They had been completed in 1937 by financier and producer Simon and Paul Soskin, who had, unhappily, been unable to redeem the mortgage to McAlpines the builders,

which had been secured to cover the cost of construction – and McAlpines foreclosed in 1939. While Maxwell speculated, J. Arthur Rank bought. Not because he wanted to use the Amalgamated Studios, but to prevent John Maxwell from acquiring them. It was simple Rank business logic – if the most modern studios in England were to be added to the Maxwell Elstree empire, there would be little hope of success for his Pinewood and new Denham Studios.

Thus in the course of three years Maxwell was prevented from making two major deals that may well have altered the face of the British film industry. It could certainly not have helped his blood pressure to pass the Amalgamated Studios every morning, knowing that Mr Rank had now leased them to the Ministry of Works, for storage purposes.

By as late as July 1939, productions were still being planned for B.I.P. Elstree. Flora Robson had made *Poison Pen*, and *The Gang's All Here*, made at Elstree and Welwyn, with Jack Buchanan, Googie Withers and Edward Everett Horton had been a tremendous success. But ironically, as summer passed into autumn and with the Amalgamated story still fresh in everyone's mind, John Maxwell was notified that in the event of hostilities his studios at Elstree would be commandeered by the Royal Ordinance Corps, for the duration of the war.

War was declared on September 3rd, 1939 and John Maxwell was to die in 1940 – it was the end of an era.

Chapter 5

War and Peace: A Fresh Start

'We did it!' Michael Redgrave as Barnes Wallis, inventor of the bouncing bomb, shares the moment of triumph with Richard Todd, playing the role of Wing Commander Guy Gibson, when positive results are finally achieved after many test failures. The highly successful *Dambusters* was produced by Robert Clark and W. A. Whittaker and directed by Michael Anderson

WAR. Gas masks, ration books, clothing coupons and dried egg epitomised the atmosphere of the time. While the public queued hungrily at the cinema for a few hours of escapism that would take their minds off the worries and dangers marking all of their lives (surely the greatest service that any entertainment industry could have offered), many British studios were commandeered by the War Office.

Elstree, the British Hollywood, played the biggest role in this production, with all of its studios being requisitioned and used in some form or another during the war. Skeleton maintenance staffs were retained at most studios, creating an even stronger camaraderie between the old hands and a comic if dramatic scenario in itself. Pinewood had been requisitioned for flour and sugar storage but, more intriguingly, had also become assigned to the Royal Mint. A wrong delivery of flour to the Elstree gates sparked off the comment, 'It may be the first time you're making money at Pinewood, mate, but we've been making dough for years.' When it was discovered that the hawk-eyed Robert Clark had been walking over a bomb on his regular B.I.P. inspections, Pinewood retaliated with the comment that he was probably making sure that it was still there.

At the time of the evacuation of the British Expeditionary Force from Dunkirk, and with B.I.P.'s film production now centred entirely at its Welwyn Studios, Brigadier G. W. Worsdell arrived at B.I.P. to take command of what was now to be the Royal Army Ordinance Corps depot, for general stores, tents, tools, domestic items and so on. His staff consisted of a sprinkling of supervisory military personnel, two platoons of girls from the Auxiliary Territorial Services, some locally recruited civilians . . . . . and Joe Grossman.

Joe had been assigned to the unsuspecting Brigadier by B.I.P. for the duration of the war and it would be hard to imagine a more unlikely partnership. If the Brigadier was to find Joe a little colourful and not altogether orthodox, in military terms, from time to time, he was also to find his help invaluable. As head of the local fire brigade it was Joe and 'his boys' who were to conduct the much needed fire-fighting course; as chief of the local St John's ambulance it was Joe and 'his boys' who could be called out in an emergency; and as 'self-appointed liaison officer', it was Joe and 'his boys' who put the B.I.P. studio cinema and film library at the army's disposal. As 'the boys' were in the main ex-studio personnel, the R.A.O.C. might have been forgiven for wondering exactly who was running the operation. But at the end of the war, the inventions and devices made at Elstree for the fake expeditionary force, used to decoy the German Air Force away from the coast of Normandy during the D-Day landing, became known to the public and Joe and 'his boys' were happy to record their pride, along with their King and country, in the work carried out by the R.A.O.C. Certainly if the War Office had been looking for a decoy for their operations, Grossman and band would have provided the perfect foil.

But with peace in 1945, came a change in the life of the studio. No longer would a caravan containing a copulating couple be released on the back lot from its breakers, to meander gently down into a crowd of extras; no more fly ripping or fake telegrams; men had been to war and the frivolous mood of the thirties was never again to be recaptured. But something else was to replace it: just as sound had altered the concept of film making in 1929, so the 1939–45 war had altered the face of the British film industry. Many of the old film hands had simply not come back, many of the established old school actors had disappeared, many of the studios had closed – and just a few had taken off to the Hollywood Hollywood, never to return. So the emphasis was on the new. New stars, new films, for a new cinema-going public and the one thing that Joe Public wanted, now more than ever after five war torn years, was his weekly treat at the cinema.

John Maxwell had always desperately hoped that on his death his family would retain control of his film empire, now the A.B.P.C. (Associated British Picture Corporation). But it was not to be. Warner Brothers acquired some family shares in the early years of the war, and in 1946 they bought a vast share bulk from the Maxwell estate, thus placing themselves in an unassailable position.

The transatlantic flavour of the British Hollywood was now more pronounced than ever. Of the old Anglo-Scots school Sir Philip Warter (John Maxwell's son-in-law) became Chairman, with Dr Eric Fletcher (afterwards Lord Fletcher) as deputy Chairman and Robert Clark Executive Director of Studios and Production. Of the new American graduates, Max Milder, head of Warner Brothers' London company and their Teddington studios, became Managing Director of A.B.P.C. and was to be succeeded by C.J. Latta, an American Warner Brothers executive. The new Anglo-American tie-up was also to mean that in principle Warner Brothers should distribute A.B.P.C. pictures in their 800 American cinemas and the Associated British would reciprocate by showing the Warner films in their British theatres. The new board was also to decide on the complete reconstruction of their Elstree Studios.

While all this was happening at the old B.I.P. now A.B.P.C. complex, the other Elstree studios were slowly getting back into gear. By 1947 the former Rock Studios, now British National, were making *The Laughing Lady* with Anne Ziegler and Webster Booth, along with *The Ghosts of Berkeley Square* with Robert Morley, Yvonne Arnaud and A.E. Matthews. The Gate Studios, by the railway, G.H.W. Productions, had been acquired by J. Arthur Rank and were involved in experimental work; they were later to be used for religious productions. G. and B. Instructional Ltd was operating from the tiny Imperial Studios next to the old B.I.P. complex and last but by no means least, the Amalgamated Studios, denied to John Maxwell but sold to the Prudential by the same J. Arthur Rank, had ironically been bought from them by M.G.M. British, who were going in for a massive overhaul to establish a miniature Culver City.

'Back to work in Britain's Hollywood' sang the *Picturegoer's* headline of 1947. The resurrection of Elstree was certainly under way. Irked at not having his own stable of stars under contract, and

From left to right, Beatrice Varley, Dulcie Gray and
Michael Denison in *My Brother Jonathan*

thus having to pay other studios for their services,
Robert Clark contacted Robert Lennard, who had
been the studio's casting director before the war,
and suggested he return to the now A.B.P.C. fold.

'Only if I can build up a new stable,' said the
forthright Lennard.

'And what makes you think that that was not
exactly what I had in mind?' came the crisp Scots
retort. Bob Lennard certainly had an almost
uncanny knack of choosing exactly the right
person to fit a role, and top directors including Fred
Zinnemann and Stanley Donen came to rely on his
unique talents.

In 1947, although the new A.B.P.C. studios were
not yet complete, the company decided to go ahead
with its first post-war production. For *My Brother
Jonathan*, based on the novel by Francis Brett
Young, they borrowed the British National Studios
across the road. Searching for a new leading man
Lennard asked Dulcie Gray if she remembered a
young man who had stood in at her test for *Banana*

Ridge at Welwyn a few years earlier.

'That shouldn't be too difficult,' she told him.
'His name is Michael Denison, he's my husband
and you can find him at home!'

My Brother Jonathan was to launch the A.B.P.C.
well on its way to reclaiming its old reputation as
number one at Elstree. It had a galaxy of new stars
to its credit – Dulcie Gray, Ronald Howard, Stephen Murray, a huge actor/farmer called James
Robertson Justice who would arrive in a gleaming
Rolls Royce with a prize pig in the back, Beatrice
Campbell and Finlay Currie. Producing a nostalgic
touch and the film was Warwick Ward, silent
heart throb of the first B.I.P. productions. His film
shot Denison to instant stardom.

***

In May 1948 the British Government reached an
agreement with Hollywood which entitled them to
take twenty-five per cent only of American earn-

91

'If that's how you feel . . . . what's it worth to you?'
Peter Brown, a deserter from the army, is discovered in
Cornwall by ex-Corporal Newman who wants 'hush
money'. A scene from the Associated British picture
Man on the Run between Derek Farr (right), as Brown,
and Kenneth More. The film was directed by Lawrence
Huntington, who also wrote the screenplay

ings out of the country. This was received with two
schools of thought. One was that it was a wonderful opportunity to recapture the American market,
since a clause in the agreement provided that for
every dollar British films were to earn in the U.S.A.
a corresponding dollar could be taken out of
Britain. The other school feared that it would be
the end of an indigenous market and that Britain
would become part of an American production
monster, who would gobble their frozen assets by
making American films in British studios for world
markets.

Perhaps with this in mind, and still waiting for
the face-lift scaffolding to be taken down at
A.B.P.C., the Boulting Brothers made *The Guinea
Pig* at the M.G.M. British studios. The story of a
poor boy who became a scholarship 'guinea-pig' at
a public school, it starred Richard Attenborough
Sheila Sim and Bernard Miles.

But at last, all was ready and in September 1948
with Vaughan N. Dean installed as the new studio
manager, *Man on the Run* became the first post-war
film to be produced at the re-built A.B.P.C. studios.
Derek Farr and Joan Hopkins were to star with
newcomers Laurence Harvey and Kenneth More
in smaller roles.

While Anna Neagle was receiving a gold medal for her performance in *Piccadilly Incident* from A.B.P.C.'s Welwyn studios, Robert Lennard was lining up another newcomer whom he had contracted to the studio, Richard Todd. He was to be given his first starring role in *The Hasty Heart*, the new studio's first international production, which was produced and directed by Vincent Sherman. Todd's co-stars were Patricia Neal and an American actor of whom a film magazine of the time wrote: '. . . . . He has never really felt like an actor at all. His real interest might lie in public service of another kind. Maybe politics. Maybe business. In which case all I can say is that he must have been a good businessman to stifle his ambition. Acting pays better!' The article, written in July 1947, referred to a gentleman by the name of Ronald Reagan.

LEFT
Patricia Neal and Ronald Reagan in *The Hasty Heart*. An article written in a 1947 film magazine had stated, 'He has never really felt like an actor at all. His real interest might lie in public service of another kind. Maybe politics . . .'

Phyllis Calvert and Richard Burton during the filming of *The Woman with No Name*

Duplicity and apprehension are expressed by Marlene Dietrich and Jane Wyman respectively in *Stagefright*, produced and directed by Alfred Hitchcock

Considering that Todd had at first declined the part of the arrogant Scottish soldier, fearing that his accent was not good enough, his Oscar nomination must have come as something of a surprise – as did the future prominence of his fellow thespian.

The cherubic old master Alfred Hitchcock was now almost permanently lost to Hollywood; but he was lured over from the States to his one-time joke-a-minute pad to produce and direct *Stagefright* for the now international studio. It starred Marlene Dietrich, Jane Wyman – the former Mrs Ronald Reagan – Michael Wilding and Richard Todd this time as the villain of the piece. Dietrich sang, in her throaty, teutonic lisp, a little number entitled *It's Simply Because I'm the Laziest Gal in Town* while swirling in another little number designed by Christian Dior. Miss Wyman however became more peeved by the moment at her own unattractive film personality and so began to improve her appearance on a day to day basis, which according

to Hitch was the reason for her failing to maintain her film character. If this was the case, then one of the final scenes must have failed abysmally, for Jane, making goo-goo eyes at Mr Wilding, looked quite delicious in an organza creation and a big picture hat.

Phyllis Calvert, who had risen to stardom along with Margaret Lockwood, Stewart Granger and James Mason, during and just after the war in the few British films that were being made, was next to star in and co-produce *Woman With No Name* with Richard Burton and Helen Cherry. This wartime psychological drama was followed by another, *Landfall*, from the novel by Nevil Shute, which introduced new A.B.P.C. starlet Patricia Plunkett and co-starred the now established Michael Denison. While the studio prepared for its biggest post war musical in 1949, Ivor Novello's *The Dancing Years*, with Dennis Price, Giselle Preville and Patricia Dainton, the funeral of the now legendary Joe Grossman, former studio manager, created a spectacle to date unsurpassed at a major British studio. Stars and film personalities congregated to pay tribute to an incredible personality and when the cortege entered Elstree village, the trail of limousines was still coming out of the studio gates

LEFT
Dennis Price and Giselle Preville in Ivor Novello's *The Dancing Years*, A.B.P.C.'s first major post-war musical. Released in 1950, it was produced by Warwick Ward and directed by Harold French

BELOW
Patricia Dainton in *The Dancing Years*

Douglas Fairbanks Junior, Greer Garson and Walter Pidgeon visiting the British Hollywood, Garson and Pidgeon to make *The Miniver Story* for M.G.M.–British, and the delightful Mr Fairbanks to commence his own production at Elstree of films for television

RIGHT
From left to right, Cesar Romero, Vera-Ellen, David Niven and Diane Hart in *Happy Go Lovely*

a mile away.

The British Hollywood was fast returning to its former glory. Now it was the turn of the M.G.M.-British Studios Ltd, at the old Amalgamated Studios. Los Angeles-style luxury and financial investment had turned the war time factory/stores back to its original format, plus. Virtually self-supporting, with its own greenhouses, restaurants, generators and garage, it was to attract its own contracted American stars as well as the cream of British film and theatre. Over the next two decades Spencer Tracy, Deborah Kerr, Robert Taylor, Elizabeth Taylor, Greer Garson, Stewart Granger, Ava Gardner, Jean Simmons, Joan Fontaine, John Gielgud, Clark Gable and many more were to grace the studio's portals.

On the A.B.P.C. stages *Captain Horatio Hornblower* for Warner Brothers, which was to star Gregory Peck, Robert Beatty and Terence Morgan, was in preparation. Lennard invited Peter Ustinov to an interview with the film's director Raoul Walsh, who was so completely amused – or bemused – by the actor's quick-fire accents and inimitable anecdotes, that it was only after he had left the studio that it was realised that Ustinov had not been offered a part.

The new British Film Production fund had been set up to administer the new Eady plan, by which a levy on cinema admissions would be channelled back into film production. In 1950 it received its first cheque of over £20,000. The plan had been instigated by the then President of the Board of Trade, Harold Wilson (later Sir Harold). Helpful as the scheme was intended to be, it was a mere spit in the ocean to A.B.P.C., who decided to sell their Welwyn Studios and concentrate on Elstree. In that year too, millionairess Lady Yule, who had owned the British National until 1948, died. Her studios were to pass briefly into other hands and then darken for several years until a new proprietor surfaced in 1952.

Meanwhile, producer Marcel Hellman, who was to become one of the elder statesmen of our British film industry, was keeping not only the dancers on their toes on the set of *Happy Go Lovely*. David

RIGHT
Sitting pretty, Vera-Ellen in the 1951 release *Happy Go Lovely*

The Magic Box is explained to H.R.H. Princess Margaret by Robert Donat during the filming. Donat played William Friese-Greene, the inventor of the first practical cinematograph camera. The film was made for the Festival of Britain in 1951

Niven, Vera-Ellen and Cesar Romero were to star in this musical about a dancer mistaken for a millionaire. The clever Mr Hellman had a very ingenious method of keeping his production on schedule. He would arrive silently on set, stare about him, produce a gold Hunter, stare at that and exit equally silently, stage left. It worked wonders. The zany Kay Kendall had a tiny part in this film, beautifully photographed by Erwin Hillier.

By now it was high time that some form of studio history was placed on film record and Gilbert Gunn devised and produced the *Elstree Story* in 1950. With a commentary by Richard Todd it contained extracts from the studio's early B.I.P. days, up to the then present time. *Blackmail, Blossom Time, Mimi, The Hasty Heart* and other milestones were

featured, and the selected sequences had been tied up, whenever possible, to make an apt and interesting comparison between old and new, resulting in an affectionate salute to the studio's past and present. Setting the scene on another stage at that time was art director Terence Verity, who was preparing *Young Wives' Tale*, a domestic comedy with husky-voiced Joan Greenwood, Nigel Patrick and Derek Farr.

A classic head on a swan's neck and enormous doe eyes had been peering from a Crookes Lacto-Calomine lotion advertisement. Its owner, young Audrey Hepburn, was spotted by Michael Denison and Dulcie Gray, dancing in a West End night club. Her gamine freshness so appealed to them, that they insisted that Robert Lennard should take a look. He did, and signed her up for *Laughter in Paradise* and *Young Wives' Tale*. A five year contract followed, and she was lent to Warner Brothers at a sum far in excess of her contract figure. Again the canny Scots accountancy was to show its mettle.

Star of the thirties and still in great form, Athene
Seyler gives tea and sympathy to newcomer Audrey
Hepburn (centre) and sexy-voiced Joan Greenwood in
Young Wives' Tale. Henry Cass directed, with
production by Victor Skutezky

For the Festival of Britain in 1951 the film doyens
decided to pool their resources and produce an
industry offering for the occasion. *The Magic Box*,
the story of inventor William Friese-Greene, was
their choice, and Robert Donat was to play the
lead. It was to be produced in and around the
A.B.P.C. studios, distributed by the Rank organisation, produced by Ronald Neame and directed by
John Boulting. Three gallant knights, Sir Laurence
Olivier, Sir Michael Redgrave and Sir Richard
Attenborough were invited to participate with
cameo appearances. Suffering as he did from
both asthma and crucifying self-doubts,
Donat the star was to run the gamut of
self-imposed fears. Was the script right?
Was he well enough to do a scene with
Laurence Olivier? And an old favourite
– was the part sympathetic enough?
With amazing tact *and* will-power,
his colleagues rallied around and
no one was too surprised when the
master craftsman turned in an excellent performance.

RIGHT
Delightful Audrey Hepburn in 1951

LEFT
Jack Hawkins (left) and Michael Denison in *Angels One Five*, the story of a wartime bomber squadron, produced by John Gossage and Derek Twist and directed by George More O'Ferrall

RIGHT
A romance set in Monte Carlo, *Twenty-Four Hours in a Woman's Life* starred (left to right) Leo Genn, Merle Oberon and Richard Todd

BELOW
Veterans A.E. Matthews and Margaret Rutherford (centre) with Helen Cherry and David Tomlinson looking at the family album in *Castle in the Air*, a comedy about a Coal Board and a rich American competing for the purchase of a poor earl's castle

While our old friend Walter Mycroft (now an independent producer based at Elstree) was making *The Woman's Angle* with director Leslie Arliss, John Maxwell's other protégé, Robert Clark, was supervising *Angels One Five* on an adjacent stage. Partly sponsored by the National Film Finance Corporation (founded in 1949 to provide film production loans), it starred Jack Hawkins, Michael Denison and Dulcie Gray and gave the new John Gregson a true chance to shine in a tale of air force heroism. Other 1951 productions were to include Merle Oberon and Leo Genn in *Twenty-Four Hours of a Woman's Life*; a dishy Richard Attenborough in *Father's Doing Fine*; and a comedy about a Coal Board and a rich American competing for the purchase of a Scottish fortress, called *Castle in the Air*. Its cast included a number of comedy favourites – David Tomlinson, Margaret Rutherford, A.E. Matthews, and Clive Morton. But Helen Cherry, the star of *Castle in the Air*, was to provide the best giggle of all. Her husband, arriving at the Elstree gate, was eyed suspiciously by a new doorman and after due deliberation was told, 'Orl right, Mr Cherry, stage four.' From then on

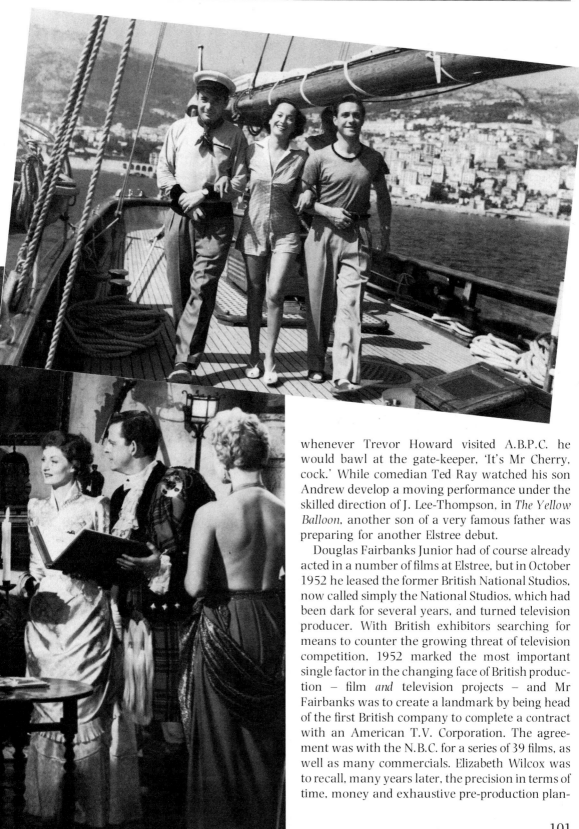

whenever Trevor Howard visited A.B.P.C. he would bawl at the gate-keeper, 'It's Mr Cherry, cock.' While comedian Ted Ray watched his son Andrew develop a moving performance under the skilled direction of J. Lee-Thompson, in *The Yellow Balloon*, another son of a very famous father was preparing for another Elstree debut.

Douglas Fairbanks Junior had of course already acted in a number of films at Elstree, but in October 1952 he leased the former British National Studios, now called simply the National Studios, which had been dark for several years, and turned television producer. With British exhibitors searching for means to counter the growing threat of television competition, 1952 marked the most important single factor in the changing face of British production – film *and* television projects – and Mr Fairbanks was to create a landmark by being head of the first British company to complete a contract with an American T.V. Corporation. The agreement was with the N.B.C. for a series of 39 films, as well as many commercials. Elizabeth Wilcox was to recall, many years later, the precision in terms of time, money and exhaustive pre-production plan-

101

ning which allowed them to produce six twenty-six minute films at the end of the first two months, with another six nearly packaged.

A.B.P.C followed in Fairbanks' footsteps shortly afterwards, but meantime the Gate studios appeared to be back in feature film fashion with Joan Fontaine and Louis Jourdan starring in *Decameron Nights*, and in answer to this star challenge M.G.M.-British were sprucing up their V.I.P. dressing-rooms for Gene Kelly's *Invitation to the Dance* and the arrival of Clark Gable and Gene Tierney to make *Never Let Me Go*.

Walt Disney was now to lend his American presence to the A.B.P.C. studios with a joint venture of *Rob Roy – The Highland Rogue*, starring Glynis Johns and Richard Todd. 'The Porridge Factory' was really to dig into its oat roots for this costume drama set in the Scottish highlands: and the plane service between Elstree and Glasgow buzzed with activity, as in good canny fashion half

RIGHT
Andrew Ray in *The Yellow Balloon*, directed by J. Lee-Thompson and produced by Victor Skutezky

Richard Attenborough surrounded by Virginia McKenna and Mary Germaine (top) and Susan Stephen and Diane Hart (below) in *Father's Doing Fine*, a comedy involving four aristocratic but impoverished sisters

of the Elstree Studios were stripped to provide technical equipment and necessities for the production. And while Mervyn Johns' daughter swirled to the highland fling, David Farrar was schooling redhead Jeanne Crain's American accent towards an English intonation. The film was *Duel in the Jungle*, an African adventure of a diamond wheeler-dealer who feigns death to collect the insurance, and co-starred Dana Andrews. On an adjoining set producer/director Mario Zampi looked as if he would be *Happy Ever After*, with his three delightful star charmers, David Niven, Yvonne de Carlo and Barry Fitzgerald.

***

Not by any stretch of the imagination could the Wilcox family have been called ordinary. Renowned director/producer Herbert, his wife star

Getting to grips with the situation are Dana Andrews and Jeanne Crain in *Duel in the Jungle*, a romantic adventure set in Africa

RIGHT
Richard Todd, Glynis Johns and James Robertson Justice in *Rob Roy – The Highland Rogue*, produced by Perce Pearce and directed by Harold French, released in 1953

104

Anna Neagle, his son John who became executive producer, and his daughter-in-law Elizabeth, a continuity expert. They will always be an integral part of the British Hollywood story that was to span over fifty years of Elstree's film history. It is not surprising, then, that Herbert was to receive a tremendous welcome from A.B.P.C. on his return to the studios in 1954 to make *Trouble in the Glen*, with Margaret Lockwood, Orson Welles and Forrest Tucker; and Anna Neagle was to receive the same ovation when she arrived for his production of *Lilacs in the Spring* with Errol Flynn.

Hell-raising, impudent, handsome Flynn was over the peak of his fabulous career by this time, but still continued to give value for money where wine, women and song were concerned, either on or off the set. He was to acquit himself extremely

LEFT
Impish Barry Fitzgerald offers a nightcap to David
Niven and Yvonne de Carlo in *Happy Ever After*, a
comedy set in Ireland

LEFT
Impish Barry Fitzgerald offers a nightcap to David
Niven and Yvonne de Carlo in *Happy Ever After*, a
comedy set in Ireland

BELOW LEFT
The Dark Avenger with Errol Flynn (left) and Peter
Finch, produced by Vaughan Dean and directed by
Henry Levin

BELOW
Anna Neagle and Errol Flynn dance the light fantastic
in *Lilacs in the Spring*: second nature to the lady, but
Flynn had to have strenuous dance instruction for the
film and he passed with flying colours

well in *King's Rhapsody* and *Lilacs in the Spring* with
some intricate dance routines and was to give one
of his last swashbuckling roles on the Elstree sets in
The Dark Avenger, with Peter Finch and Joanne
Dru.

Blockbuster, but with a dam was to be Robert
Clark's own special production. *The Dam Busters*
were, in fact, a special squadron out to destroy the
Ruhr Dams, during the Second World War. Based
on the actual war records the film starred Michael
Redgrave as Barnes Wallis, the inventor of the
'Bouncing Bomb', which was eventually to do the
trick, and Richard Todd as Wing Commander Guy
Gibson, commanding officer of the 617 Squadron.
It was also to do the trick at the box office.

Contrast was certainly the order of the day in the
fifties. Well received from the critics was Kenneth
Harper's production of *For Better For Worse*, a

107

domestic comedy with Dirk Bogarde and Susan
Stephen as dotty newlyweds; while Warner Brothers were to pull the stops out with *Moby Dick*.

It was to be the costumed *Jaws* of its day,
produced and directed by the great John Huston
and photographed by Oswald Morris. The classic
story of Captain Ahab stalking the great whale that
had taken off one of his legs starred Gregory Peck
as the former and a derelict schooner in a sturdy
rubber wrapping to resemble the latter. In a storm
it got away and the shipping authorities that
evening warned all shipping in the area to be on
the look-out for a white rubber whale.

By the mid-fifties there had been very few
changes in the A.B.P.C. board cast list, although
Jimmy Wallis was now assistant to Robert Clark
and Stanley Black had been appointed musical
director of the studio.

Robert Lennard was still the casting director and
John Mills and Cecil Parker were chosen to play the
leads in *It's Great to be Young* by Ted Willis. But
even the fey Mr Lennard could not have foreseen
that the role of managing director of the studios
was awaiting a young organ salesman in the film,
by the name of Bryan Forbes. But no E.S.P. was
needed to divine the special quality of
Anneliese Rothenberger's voice in the
Michael Powell and Emeric Pressburger
production of *Oh . . . Rosalinda!*,
A.B.P.C.'s first cinemascope feature.
Based on Johann Strauss's *Die Fleder-
maus*, it included Michael Redgrave,
Mel Ferrer, the gorgeous Ludmilla
Tcherina, Anthony Quayle and Anton
Walbrook, in a spectacle about old Vienna in the
naughty nineties.

TOP RIGHT
There's *Trouble in the Glen*, with Margaret Lockwood
attractively placed between the towering charms of
Orson Welles and Forrest Tucker. The film was
directed and produced by Herbert Wilcox

RIGHT
Captain Ahab (Gregory Peck) in search of the great
whale *Moby Dick* which had devoured one of his legs
on a previous encounter

ABOVE
Bryan Forbes has a nice line in sales patter, but Cecil Parker seems unconvinced in *It's Great To Be Young*, produced by Victor Skutezky and directed by Cyril Frankel

BELOW
The great John Huston discusses the problems of the day with a young film extra during his production of *Moby Dick*. Huston also directed

ABOVE
John Mills livens things up a bit in *It's Great To Be Young*

ANYONE SPEAKING
TO
MADAME TCHERINA
IN FRENCH
WILL BE LIABLE TO A

Although there was to be a welcome new addition to the British Hollywood studio scene in the fifties – the New Elstree Studios, built by the Danziger brothers for mainly American T.V. productions – a chilling and realistic note in Peter Noble's *The British Film and Television Year Book* of 1955/56 warned that 'The following studios are no longer active in film production, either temporarily or permanently: Highbury, Islington, Lime Grove, Teddington, Isleworth, Welwyn, Denham, Ealing, Riverside, Wembley.'

After watching television in 1933, Sam Goldwyn was to prophesy that within three years every home would turn into a private kinema. A war and old traditions had slowed the British conversion, but the late starter was preparing for a neck and neck finish with the British film industry. As it became clear to the A.B.P.C. board that Independent Television was to become a reality in Britain, they decided to enter the stakes and in 1955 were awarded the contracts for the Midlands and Northern programmes on Saturdays and Sundays. A.B.C. Television Ltd selected the Teddington Studios as its main base for production and administration, and the A.B.P.C. Elstree film studio would now start to make television productions with its Teddington sister company, along with its own complement of feature film projects.

And in 1955 at the British Hollywood, that complement was still very demanding. Britain's sex bomb of the fifties was Diana Dors, a busty, long-legged blonde, whose acting talents had been played down in favour of her physical attributes by many of the critics. But *Yield to the Night*, the story of a woman in the condemned cells, recalling her past, was to change all that. Diana was to surprise even the toughest dilettante with an exceptionally fine performance and was supported by such other top calibre actresses as Yvonne Mitchell, Mona Washbourne and Marianne Stone.

In stark contrast, the comedy *My Wife's Family* was being set up on an adjoining stage. Having

The all-star cast of *Oh Rosalinda* includes such talented beauties as Anneliese Rothenberger and Ludmilla Tcherina whilst Britain, France, U.S.A. and Russia are represented in the shapes of Dennis Price, Michael Redgrave, Mel Ferrer and Anthony Quayle; Anton Walbrook is no doubt the masked stranger. Michael Powell and Emeric Pressburger, as well as some of the personnel responsible for the film's success, are also shown

Victor Mature grasping his opportunity with Eric Pohlman in *Interpol*

Diana Dors, a busty long-legged blonde, whose acting talents were played down in favour of her physical attributes by many critics

It may be dead, but it won't lie down: the quicksilver with of comedian Ted Ray (right) and Ronald Shiner looks lost on Greta Gynt and headgear in *My Wife's Family*

Yield to the Night, produced by Kenneth Harper and directed by J. Lee-Thompson, showed Diana Dors to be an actress of depth and sensitivity in the role of a woman in the condemned cell, recalling the events that led to her death sentence

already had two very successful runs in 1931 and 1941, A.B.P.C. decided that third time might be even luckier. The second-to-none wit, Ted Ray was to co-star with Ronald Shiner, with Greta Gynt, Robertson Hare and Diane Hart in supporting roles.

Other 1955 productions were to include *Now and Forever* with Janette Scott, Kay Walsh, Jack Warner, Pamela Brown and Sonia Dresdel; and by the time the undulating Anita Ekberg, Victor Mature and Trevor Howard had chased or been chased by a gang of dope smugglers in *Interpol*; and the studio had made two more musicals: *The Good Companions* with Eric Portman and Celia Johnson, and *Let's Be Happy* with Tony Martin, Vera-Ellen and Robert Flemyng (the story of a poor aristocrat in pursuit of an American girl, whom he believes to be loaded) – the British film industry was trying to sort out its own warp from its woof.

The President of the British Film Producers Association, Sir Henry French, drew attention to the fact that no revision of entertainments duty had been granted since 1945 and expanded the

Tony Martin and Vera-Ellen in the musical *Let's Be Happy*, produced by Marcel Hellman, directed by Henry Levin

BELOW
Anna Neagle with husband/director Herbert Wilcox and Janette Scott on the set of *The Lady is a Square*

discussion by pointing out that films made in Britain by a subsidiary of an American company were classed as British in levy terms and therefore eligible for payments from that duty. Michael Powell wrote that the major British distributors were as fond of the independent producers as they were of leprosy. Ian Dalrymple suggested that 'Our film future lies in Europe', while Herbert Wilcox stated unequivocally that Wardour Street lacked drive and imagination.

But Mr Wilcox, however, did not. In 1958 he produced and directed Anna Neagle and the new dreamboat singer Frankie Vaughan in *The Lady is a Square*. The film also 'discovered' a young man who was constantly being rediscovered or just recovered, but who in fact had already been in show business for a number of years, Anthony Newley.

With the success of the Frank Godwin/Ted Willis production of *Woman in a Dressing Gown*, both critically and at the Berlin Film Festival, two international actresses were preparing their wardrobes for a trip to the British Hollywood. Both had

A distraught Yvonne Mitchell as the *Woman in a Dressing Gown* lets fly at attractive Sylvia Syms, with Anthony Quayle as the reluctant spectator. J. Lee-Thompson directed this prize-winning drama

RIGHT
Lady without any sort of gown, Carole Lesley was under contract to A.B.P.C. during the fifties and appeared in a number of Elstree films, including *Woman in a Dressing Gown*

Ingrid Bergman and Cary Grant in the comedy
Indiscreet, produced by Cary Grant and Stanley Donen
and directed by Stanley Donen

RIGHT
Star reel: Ingrid Bergman dances with Cecil Parker
while Phyllis Calvert and Cary Grant keep time in
Indiscreet

delightful accents, one Italian, the other Swedish.
Both were sensual in different ways; both had hit
the headlines over motherhood problems; one
because she could not have a baby (but happily,
subsequently did), the other by producing a child
in circumstances that at that time created hypo-
critical outrage. Both were top money-making
stars of their day. Sophia Loren and Ingrid
Bergman. Sophia's film with William Holden,
Trevor Howard and Oscar Homolka was called *The
Key* and did not fare well at the box office; but
Ingrid's film with Cary Grant, *Indiscreet*, about a
diplomat pretending to be married in order to avoid
the tender trap, produced the usual queue of
Bergman/Grant admirers at the cinemas.

If the Christmas toasts towards the end of the
fifties at Elstree were to begin with 'to absent
friends', the war and its deprivations were fast
receding in people's minds and lives. Luxurious
food, clothes and cars were now in evidence and
the people of Elstree were once again blasé about
the stars and producers who set foot in their village
shops. And the new A.B.P.C. studios had suc-

George Baker (centre) as the swashbuckling adventurer in *The Moonraker*, an A.B.P.C. picture which co-starred Sylvia Syms, Marius Goring and Clive Morton, released in 1958

RIGHT
John Mills and Sylvia Syms look anything but *Ice Cold in Alex*, a war-time adventure produced by W. A. Whittaker and directed by J. Lee-Thompson

BELOW
Sophia Loren and Trevor Howard in *The Key*

LEFT
Kirk Douglas (centre) listens cheerfully to Burt Lancaster's complaints in *The Devil's Disciple*

BELOW LEFT
Laurence Olivier and Mervyn Johns in *The Devil's Disciple*

RIGHT
The combined ages of these three superstars, Sybil Thorndike (centre), Kathleen Harrison (right) and Estelle Winwood totalled 211 years at the time of *Alive and Kicking*, released in 1958

BELOW
Rock 'n' roll hero Tommy Steele in *Tommy the Toreador*, with Janet Munro, Sidney James and Bernard Cribbins

ceeded in what they had set out to do, creating new films and stars for the ever-hungry distributors and public. Walter Mycroft died in 1959, but John Maxwell's other right hand, Robert Clark, was still firmly in charge of studio production. Although the threat of television competition must have been staring him squarely in the eye, he finished the decade with some excellent productions. For the special effects of one of these, *Ice Cold in Alex*, George Blackwell had to produce four hundredweight of soggy rice pudding in the middle of the desert to simulate a bog-type morass; a fact that did not detract in the slightest from the uproar caused by the sight of Miss Sylvia Syms' cleavage being pressed to a panting John Mills.

The Devil's Disciple, with Burt Lancaster, Kirk Douglas, Laurence Olivier and Janette Scott followed in 1959; and then there were the three old ladies . . . . not locked anywhere in fact but *Alive and Kicking*. Their combined ages totalled 211 years, but they were in their studio make-up chairs every morning at seven-thirty and were required

Script conference with the author of *Look Back In Anger*, John Osborne (right). Claire Bloom thoughtfully makes a point to Richard Burton and Mary Ure

to sing, dance, climb, fish and drive a speedboat, all of which they did with superb professionalism. They were Dame Sybil Thorndike, Kathleen Harrison and Estelle Winwood.

Rock and roll hero Tommy Steele had his fans squealing with teenage joy at the studio gates during the filming of *Tommy the Toreador*, directed by John Paddy Carstairs, while Professor Jimmy Edwards and Arthur Howard were contending with their pupils in *Bottoms Up*, traditional comedy fare. But it was now becoming clear that a new school of film maker was emerging. *Look Back in Anger*, written by John Osborne, brought to Elstree by executive producer Harry Saltzman and directed by Tony Richardson, was a perfect example of this genre. The story of a frustrated working-class intellectual, it starred Richard Burton, Claire Bloom and Mary Ure and was to signal many changes between the established type of film entertainment and the new-look, realistic, modern film drama.

The signals then for the approaching sixties were not Stop, Wait and Go, but Change. With Gordon L.T. Scott's production of *Look Back in Anger* collecting critical bouquets and A.B.P.C. embarking on a powerful film and television line-up, one would have had to have been blind, deaf and dumb, not to have seen the changing image – and many of us were.

You paid your money – and you took your chance.

Chapter 6
Pop Go the Sixties

Crowds of teenagers turned up at the A.B.P.C. studio gates to welcome rock 'n' roll star Cliff Richard, seen here with the Shadows in *The Young Ones*

OVER thirty years earlier it had been Warwick Ward or Jameson Thomas whose smile was enough to send the damsels into genteel raptures and reach for their smelling salts. The sixties were to provide Joe Brown, Tommy Steele, Frank Ifield, Marty Wilde and Cliff Richard, whose fans were about as delicate as Roscoe 'Fatty' Arbuckle in *Les Sylphides*. The new heart-throbs were all young, groovy . . . . . and loud, and their trademarks were a brilliantined quiff, a guitar and a hip-twitching action that was designed to dislocate the lumbar region and trousers alike. Be that as it may, they were adored – and in many cases still are – and made a lot of money for themselves, their producers and the studios.

In the topsy-turvy world of the early sixties, the British film studios and producers certainly needed all of their wits about them to combat, let alone comprehend, the changes that were taking place. Television competition was not only having its effect on box office takings, but was in turn producing its own heroes and fashion; and 'eyes down' Bingo calls and Tenpin Bowling Clubs were being introduced as the main features in some of the now redundant cinemas. To add insult to injury at the beginning of the decade, and in the middle of yet another film production crisis, the government announced the go-ahead for a three-year trial period of 'pay' T.V.

But the old Porridge Factory was not about to lose its equilibrium. Along with their Warner

123

Brothers partners, the old rear guard of the A.B.P.C. board set up a new line of action, to take on the new, develop what was best of the old and, perhaps most important of all, open up the studios still more for independent productions wanting to use the studios for both feature and television films. After all, in 1960 A.B.P.C. still had 319 cinemas to fill and they set to work with a will.

So while Jack L. Warner was cementing Anglo-American relations by presenting A.B.P.C. chairman Sir Philip Warter with a personal cheque for the British Cinematograph Trade Benevolent Fund, and Warners man C.J. Latta as managing director of A.B.P.C. was signing up the screen rights for Willis Hall's *The Long and the Short and the Tall*, Peter Finch was busy acquiring a couple of stone for the title role in *The Trials of Oscar Wilde*. Sheer madness, muttered the critics, to cast a handsome, wiry Australian as a corpulent, Irish homosexual. There was more to come. The news broke that Robert Morley, who had made a tremendous hit on Broadway in the stage play, was going to play the role of Wilde in a rival film production. In the end it was Morley's version that was to win the production race, while Finch's masterly interpretation walked away with the acting accolades.

By now *The Long and the Short and the Tall* was well into production on stage three, under the direction of a man whose association with the

Lord Alfred Douglas (John Fraser, centre) looks on with considerable embarrassment as his father, the Marquis of Queensberry (Lionel Jeffries) presents Oscar Wilde (Peter Finch) with a bouquet of rotting vegetables. A tense scene from *The Trials of Oscar Wilde*, produced by Harold Huth and directed by Ken Hughes

RIGHT
The Long and the Short and the Tall starring Richard Harris and Laurence Harvey

Comedian Tony Hancock and silver-tongued George Sanders on the set of *The Rebel*, an A.B.P.C. production released in 1961 and directed by Robert Day

studio was both long and prestigious, British producer/director and former editor Leslie Norman. His stars in this Michael Balcon production – a tale of moral and personality clashes within an army patrol in war torn Malaya – were Laurence Harvey, Richard Todd and Richard Harris. A less than orthodox character, Harris would disappear from time to time to fortify himself against the hazards of war. Lots would be drawn amongst the younger crew members to see who would be nominated to nip across to the pub to request his presence back to the battle zone. On one such occasion the patrol returned from the pub an hour later, without so much as a slur to their lips or an unsteady gait between them, but bearing the body of a totally bombed young crew-runner on their shoulders.

While no one could deny the strong American

influence on A.B.P.C., it must be said that the studios undoubtedly gave a tremendous boost to British talent in the sixties – and not only to the aforementioned actors and young songsters. British television personalities and comics were to be given enormous opportunities to develop and shine in feature films, in accordance with a policy very akin to the studios' system of the thirties of developing the music hall talent of the day.

Former Windmill comedian Tony Hancock, considered by many to be one of the greatest comics of all time, with his sad spaniel-like countenance and superb sense of timing, starred in the A.B.P.C. production of *The Rebel*. In the film he portrayed a city gent who rebels against his suburban cage and decides to become a beatnik Parisian painter. Like so many 'funny' men he was an intense worrier whose work could spark off a bout of deep depres-

sion, and it was not unknown for Hancock to keep his director, crew and fifty extras all dressed in city gear, waiting on a Waterloo platform. He would arrive with a breathless, 'Sorry I'm late, but I've been up all night worrying about the film,' when everyone knew that he had spent the tortured wee hours trying not to.

But much of this British patronage would not have been possible without the American presence, and A.B.P.C. next opened its British Hollywood doors and coffers to three American majors. Michael Anderson's *The Naked Edge*, Gary Cooper's last film, with Michael Wilding, Deborah Kerr and Diane Cilento, was made for United Artists; *Lolita*, directed by Stanley Kubrick, the story of the teenage temptress, played by Sue Lyon, who so ensnares a middle-aged professor (James Mason) that he marries her mother (Shelley Winters) just

LEFT
Vivien Leigh and Warren Beatty during the shooting of *The Roman Spring of Mrs Stone*

RIGHT
Eric Portman looks on as Deborah Kerr and Gary Cooper plan their next move in crime thriller *The Naked Edge*

'Hello, my darlings.' Comedian Charlie Drake, escorted by two belles from the harem in *Sands of the Desert*, greets visitor to the set Robert Mitchum

to be near her, for M.G.M.; and Shirley MacLaine's handsome twenty-three-year-old brother, Warren Beatty, who looked as if he was well qualified to join the Hollywood star set, appeared with Vivien Leigh in *The Roman Spring of Mrs Stone*, for Warner Brothers.

In the meantime, a number of new directors were being appointed to the A.B.P.C. board, including the founder's son Erik Maxwell, and Howard Thomas, managing director of A.B.C. Television Ltd. The corporation also went on to buy back a number of the shares owned by Warner Brothers and to form a joint distribution company between Associated British-Pathe and Warner Brothers, which was christened Warner-Pathe Distributors. The new company was to handle the films from Warners' Burbank studios and A.B.P.C.'s Elstree studios, and those of Allied Artists.

Although A.B.P.C., and M.G.M. up the road, were steaming ahead with full studios, there were to be two sad feature film production casualties. A.T.V. Television acquired the former Blattner Rock/British National Studios and had their official opening in 1962, and Andrew Smith Harkness had long since taken over the former Gate, Rank owned studios by the railway. While being totally complementary to the new era, A.T.V. was to bring in a lot of business to the A.B.P.C. Studios and Harkness (Europe's leading big screen manufacturers) were to take it out, so to speak. But their arrival was to signal the initial disintegration of the British Hollywood.

What could have been more appropriate, then, at this time, than the appearance of Drake, a national hero? Well, two Drakes, in fact – Sir Francis . . . . and Charlie. The former, alias Terence Morgan, had changed his image somewhat to appear in twenty-six episodes for I.T.C., a sister company of A.T.V.; the latter of 'Hello my darlins' fame, to baby-face his way through two comedies that were to be produced by Gordon Scott for A.B.P.C., *Sands of the Desert* and *Petticoat Pirates*.

Tiny, chubby Charlie Drake, who had wowed them in the aisles as a bewildered little electrician, covered in balloons, cowering from a vindictive knife thrower, adored all that money and fame were to bring him, including champagne, luscious ladies and an enormous voiture; pinched for speeding he hoisted himself back on to his sliding cushions, fixed his huge forget-me-nots from under golden curls on to the copper in question and ventured sweetly, 'Hi'm so sorry hofficcicer, but I couldn't see hover the top of the wheel.'

To complete the hat trick Kenneth Harper was to produce Robert Morley and Dave King in *Go to Blazes*, a comedy about some unsuccessful crooks who become firemen in preparation for their next 'job'. Bob Lennard signed up two new stars for this production: Maggie Smith, 'a lady with an incredible eye for character detail' and a young man called Daniel Massey, whom he felt could become a younger edition of Rex Harrison. Certainly if Mr Massey's theatrical family background was anything to go by – actor father Raymond Massey, actress mother Adrienne Allen and actress sister Anna Massey – that confidence was well founded.

With Peter Ustinov well into the production of *Billy Budd*, which was to give his Cockney dis-

Daniel Massey and Maggie Smith in the 1961 A.B.P.C. comedy *Go to Blazes*

covery Terence Stamp his first big break, teenage crowds were beginning to form outside the A.B.P.C. gates for the arrival of Cliff Richard.

Admitting that he didn't know a rock from a roll, was to prove no handicap to Sidney Furie, the director of the musical *The Young Ones*, in which Cliff was to star with Robert Morley. This unusual piece of casting was to pay off. Richard, backed by the Shadows, played a youth club leader, with the marvellous Morley, backed by old school snobbery, as his unsympathetic Pater. The film was to attract both *The Young Ones* and their parents to the box office. The film also owed much to choreographer Herb Ross, who taught the company how to make a musical.

Meanwhile the comment amongst the cast of *The Pot Carriers*, a story of prison life, was that the film was to be released in July and the director three years later. Director Peter Graham Scott responded with the quip that if there was any further insubordination, the cast would not be allowed out of their cells until the end of shooting. Managing to be less ruthless on another stage, producer/director Val Guest was putting *Jigsaw* together, with the help of his lovely leading lady Yolande Donlan, the tale of a married man being slowly tracked down for the murder of his mistress.

With the boom in production and the loss of two

Accused of cowardice on failing to get fresh supplies to a beleaguered English garrison, Sir Francis Drake (Terence Morgan) seeks a private audience with Queen Elizabeth I (Jean Kent). From a television series made by I.T.C. Entertainment, *Sir Francis Drake*

Peter Ustinov and Terence Stamp in *Billy Budd*

local studios (hence no overflow facilities), A.B.P.C. decided to invest heavily in their own studios. It was now the turn of M.G.M. to look wistfully down the road as 'the old Porridge Factory' was fitted for its new finery. New stages, cutting rooms, ancillary services, underground car park, restaurant, movie-history museum and office block were planned and commenced with a mid-sixties completion date in mind. There was to be one more jewel in the A.B.P.C. crown in the early sixties that was to be the envy of every other studio in the U.K. as well as many abroad: its Film Library. This invaluable collection of stock shots, features, stills, sound effects and music represented the amalgamation of material from eight sources. All A.B.P.C. material from their own Elstree and past Welwyn studios, the Ealing collection (which they had purchased on the studio's closure), Anglo Amalgamated, A.B.C. T.V., various T.V. series and the old Warner Brothers and B.I.P. libraries.

Providing a proud and nostalgic forty-year link with those B.I.P. films and his father, director Captain Walter Summers, son Jeremy Summers took the floor to direct *The Punch and Judy Man*, with Tony Hancock, Sylvia Syms, Ronald Fraser and Barbara Murray. Hancock, playing a man whose marriage and livelihood are on the decline, showed new dramatic dimensions to his fans, who nevertheless preferred to typecast him as the most successful British comedian of the day – which he was.

Two other light entertainers longing to play 'heavies' were Tommy Steele, who had already had a great success at the Old Vic, and Cliff Richard, who was yearning to play Heathcliff in *Wuthering Heights*. He was going to have to wait a long time, for following the success of *The Young Ones*, Cliff and the Shadows were now the heart-throbs of the day, who could reduce an audience of normally sensible girls to screaming, handkerchief-biting, sobbing hysteria. If Clara Bow had been the 'It' girl of the twenties, then Mr Richard was undoubtedly the 'It' boy of the sixties.

Never slow on the uptake, A.B.P.C. launched an even more ambitious musical, *Summer Holiday*. It was to be an even greater success than its predecessor; produced by Ken Harper, its associate

RIGHT
The Saint, a television series from I.T.C. Entertainment, starred Roger Moore, seen here getting his cards in the company of Goldilocks (Joyce Blair)

producer was Andrew Mitchell, another gentleman who was to become familiar with the managing director's chair, some years hence.

But in no way was television to be neglected. Handsome, dashing daredevils were needed just as much for the small screen as for the large, and handsome dashing Roger Moore was there to fill the bill for Leslie Charteris's hero in *The Saint*. A series of seventy-one episodes, it was to provide a wonderful run-in for this courteous, professional star, who was to go on to make such a hit in feature films.

Just as well, though, that he stayed away from the Old Bailey set next door, where a positively evil *Dr Crippen* was packing enough menace into one glance to frighten the hardiest of private investigators and even Coral Browne and Samantha Eggar were finding it difficult to equate the likable Donald Pleasence with the not-so-pleasant doctor.

Still following the thirties pattern of a star system, musicals, comedies and screen idols, Elstree also continued to play host to numerous producers from abroad. But whereas in the pre-war days they had come in the main from the Continent, in the sixties they were also to arrive from the United States. They included such great names as Kubrick, Huston, Zampi, Zinnemann and Joseph Losey, who was to win international acclaim with *The Servant*, with part A.B.P.C. backing, although the film was not made at Elstree.

Also just returned from the States was a suave, silver tongued British actor called George Sanders, who played bounders to perfection and who had

Barbara Windsor measures out the bangers for the other *Crooks in the Cloisters*. An A.B.P.C. comedy produced by Gordon L. T. Scott and directed by Jeremy Summers, it also starred Bernard Cribbins, Davy Kaye and Ronald Fraser

been lost to the States for many years. He added a subtle touch of class to several A.B.P.C. comedies. Having smoothed away any rough edges on *The Rebel*, he next turned his attention to Charlie Drake in *The Cracksman*. It was delightful casting, for this unlikely pair struck sparks from each other, ably assisted by Nyree Dawn Porter and Dennis Price. Sanders always maintained that when life no longer held any pleasure for him, he would give it up, as indeed he did, to the sorrow of his many devoted fans.

Bounding on, however, into a further spate of comedies and musicals, Ray Galton and Alan Simpson wrote the screenplay for *The Bargee* with Harry H. Corbett and Eric Sykes; Barbara Windsor and Ronald Fraser starred in *Crooks in the Cloisters*; and director Ken Russell made his feature film debut with the comedy *French Dressing*.

What a Crazy World, you might think, but it was certainly a profitable one. The kids did indeed go crazy over this musical which featured a number of their rock and roll favourites: Joe Brown, a blonde, perky Cockney with a big grin, Marty Wilde, Freddie and the Dreamers, the Bruvvers and the Happy Wanderers.

Chairman Sir Philip Warter was happy to announce the highest profits ever for the A.B.P.C. group in 1964. 'Boom time for Elstree' sang the

A matter of life and death for Mrs Peel (Diana Rigg), whose life is in the hands of immaculate hero Steed (Patrick MacNee) in *The Avengers*, an A.B.C. Television production.

trade headlines, though it could just as well have been 'Bloom Time For Elsie' as long as Cliff Richard was singing it. For while Alan Bates was offering *Nothing but the Best* to Millicent Martin in a black comedy directed by Clive Donner, Cliff was busy being coached by dancer Gillian Lynne for another Elstree spectacular, *Wonderful Life*. It was also to star Walter Slezak, Susan Hampshire, Una Stubbs, Richard O'Sullivan and the Shadows in a tale of a pop group cast away on a tropical island, where they encounter a film group on location and subsequently become stars. A tiny part in the film

was also given to Miss Israel (Aliza Gur), now married to Sheldon Schrager, Vice-President in Charge of Production for Columbia Pictures Inc., Burbank. It was to be another blockbuster for smash hit Cliff, who by this time had also become an accomplished dancer.

If the 'Brits' were to hold sway in the first half of the sixties in the British Hollywood, then the 'Yanks' were to remind their hosts of their presence and expertise. A.B.P.C.'s American managing director, C.J. Latta, was awarded the C.B.E. for his public services: he had founded the Variety

Cliff Richard and Susan Hampshire in *Wonderful Life*

ABOVE

Distinguished costumiers Bermans and Nathans showed that it's not what you do, it's the way that you do it, by simply taking a doe skin and stretching it across their model. The fact that the model in *One Million Years B.C.* was beautiful Raquel Welch simplified the task enormously

LEFT

Christopher Lee Looks on with trepidation as Ursula Andress bares her bosom in *She*. A Hammer production by Michael Carreras, with Robert Day directing

135

Frank Ifield sings to four lovely maids in *Up Jumped a Swagman*, produced by Andrew Mitchell and directed by Christopher Miles

Club of Great Britain in 1949 and under his guidance one and a half million pounds had been raised from all sides of show business, for sick and needy children. Miss Tallulah Bankhead, making a brief but gusty visit to Elstree, growled 'Where's the elevator?' on surveying a few steps to her dressing room, having already been dubbed 'Miss Astoffolees' for having broken all speed regulations on the Elstree lot in her HEL 777 Rolls. It still looked as if the Anglo/American entente was set for some time to come.

All the same, nothing could have been more British than a city gentleman, complete with bowler hat, immaculate umbrella and a crinkly intelligence behind the eyes, who was to set many a heart a flutter and yet entertain at the same time. He was Steed, alias Patrick MacNee, of *The Avengers*, a sophisticated, tongue-in-cheek, thriller series for A.B.C. Television, that was to shoot to the top of the charts and was to have a series of leading ladies whose cool cultured beauty was contrasted with and complemented by their gorgeously trendy gear and judo expertise. They were Honor Blackman, Diana Rigg and Linda Thorson.

Industries are rarely able to pinpoint the reasons for a change in atmosphere and fashion. World events and a search for new themes are always contributing factors. By the mid-sixties the mood was beginning to veer away from the musical and the comedy, towards the prehistoric and horrific, with lashings of sly humour. So while the spine-chilling Vincent Price was preparing to hypnotise his victims and his audiences in the Nat Cohen/Stuart Levy production of *The Masque of the Red Death*, Hammer Films settled themselves very nicely into their A.B.P.C. studio lair and proceeded to make a bomb out of both. They also had an eye for two of the most beautiful and hedonistic ladies of the period. The first was Ursula Andress, the veritable goddess of pin-ups, who was to star with Peter Cushing in a tale of reincarnation and revenge in *She*, and twin-sister type, blonde, lithe and pouting Raquel Welch. Monty Berman, head of Bermans and Nathans, one of the oldest and distinguished costumiers in the business, was to recall with understandable pleasure, how he faced the task of putting clothes on the Hammer glamour. Miss Welch had such a perfect body that for *One Million Years B.C.* Bermans took a soft doe skin, stretched it across her, tied it together with thongs, glued tiny pieces of fur around the edges and hey presto, a devastating prehistoric lady. Proving yet again the old adage that it's not what you do, it's the way that you do it.

Also showing the way to do it was American Ray Harryhausen, in whose brilliant hands pre-historic monster models came to life, and British Les Bowie who created the world for the film in six days on a slender budget.

After three more spine chillers – *The Fearless Vampire Killers* directed by Roman Polanski with the ill-starred Sharon Tate; *The Double Man* starring Yul Brynner and Britt Ekland; and *Theatre of Death* in which Evelyn Laye was to have a guest appearance – it was time for some light relief. It was to appear in the form of *Mr Ten Per Cent* with Charlie Drake, George Baker, Derek Nimmo and John le Mesurier in a tale of an unscrupulous impresario, who is looking for a guaranteed 'flop' to write off as a tax loss; and *Up Jumped a Swagman*, filmed at the M.G.M. studios down the road, starring Australian Frank Ifield (of the golden larynx) and Suzy Kendall, and produced by Andrew Mitchell.

Despite the heady production boom at the A.B.P.C. studios and M.G.M.-British up the road still working to full capacity, admissions to U.K. cinemas in 1966 had dropped to a weekly average of six million, compared with 6.9 million in 1965 and 8.1 million in 1964. Realising that there was a need for diversification, A.B.P.C.'s chairman Sir Philip Warter had already restructured the organisation. The new composition of the organisation by 1966 was: Associated British Picture Corporation, Associated British Productions, Associated British Cinemas Ltd, Associated British Pathe Ltd, Pathe Laboratories Ltd, and A.B.C. Television Ltd.

By early 1967 the new studio building programme was almost complete. It needed to be. In addition to the Associated British Productions, with Robert Clark as its chief executive and Jimmy Wallis as its managing director, such companies as Hammer films, Anglo-Amalgamated, headed by Nat Cohen, and Elstree Distributors were all utilising the studios, as well as A.B.C. and I.T.C., who were making television programmes.

To christen the new dressing rooms Bette Davis arrived for *The Anniversary*, the story of an emasculating mother of three sons, who assemble on the anniversary of their parents' wedding. For the character of a woman slowly destroying her offspring's lives with intent and purpose Miss Davis was required to wear an eye patch, which affected both her balance and temperament on set. But the studios were quite used to working with this star quality. A stickler for accuracy, Miss Davis had insisted during a former production, *The Nanny*, on searching for and wearing exactly the right sinister and masculine nurse's uniform for the role, but had been furious when she had been complimented on her attractive appearance by a visitor to the set! Professional to her finger tips, she 'tub-thumped' both films on a television show some time later and presented her host with an eye patch, with the famous Davis deadpan flutter.

Surrounded by her family, possessive mother Bette Davis raises her glass in *The Anniversary*

ABOVE
Hildergarde Neff and Eric Porter look a little lost themselves in *The Lost Continent*, first shown in 1968

RIGHT
'Crash, bang, wallop – what a picture!' Tommy Steele and Julia Foster in the big number line-up of *Half a Sixpence*, based on the H. G. Wells story *Kipps*

Thriller writer Dennis Wheatley, meanwhile, had the pleasure of seeing two of his novels being filmed simultaneously on adjoining sets, by the house of Hammer: *The Devil Rides Out* with Christopher Lee and Charles Gray and *The Lost Continent* with Eric Porter and Hildegarde Neff. An especially large special effects department was set up for the latter, a fantasy about a tramp steamer drifting into a seaweed land of monsters. Several scorpions were purchased to enlarge on camera as possible prehistoric/fantasy monsters. They managed to wander off from their tank one warm night and the studios were left to ponder why the stills department had taken to rushing about in thick gloves and wellingtons.

In October 1967 Robert Clark gave a glittering reception on A.B.P.C. stage eight for Herbert Wilcox and Anna Neagle, to mark the publication of the former's autobiography and their long association with the studio. The A.B.P.C. board, stars and distinguished guests, including Sir Lewis Casson, Lord Brabourne, and Lord Hinchinbrooke assembled to pay tribute to this remarkable pair. True to form, the ever professional Dame Anna (as she was to become in 1969) had to leave the party ahead of time, for her evening performance in the West End success, *Charlie Girl*.

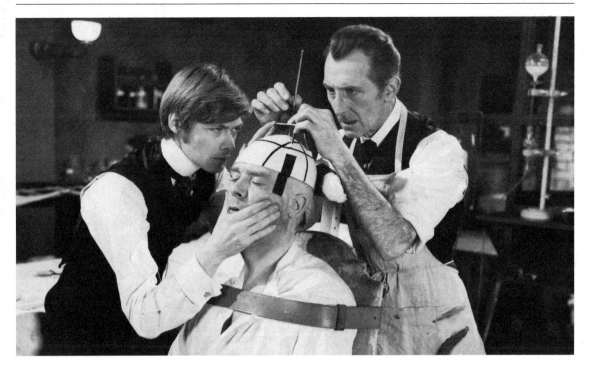

Simon Ward and Peter Cushing concentrate on a delicate piece of surgery in *Frankenstein Must Be Destroyed*

But even as the A.B.P.C. champagne corks were popping, Wardour Street nostrils were beginning to quiver with the scent of a possible industry take-over bid that would mean a momentous change for all the British Hollywood, and the A.B.P.C. studios in particular. For the moment, though, business was to continue as usual with Tommy Steele giving a superbly polished performance in the musical *Half a Sixpence*, which had been partly shot at Elstree for Paramount; and the arrival of superstar Elizabeth Taylor, Robert Mitchum, Mia Farrow and Peggy Ashcroft, for the *Secret Ceremony*, a film that was to have a cold British box office but sound American success, as well as a divided critical reception. For while Dick Richards of the *Daily Mirror* was to write about a '. . . murky, moody old load of psychological rubbish', Derek Malcolm of the *Guardian* was extolling its virtues with such comments as '. . . . quite beautifully made . . . decorated with elegant precision . . .' and so on.

Even so, by the time Robert Clark was finalising a new Hammer production deal at the A.B.P.C. studios, the take-over whispers and rumours had

LEFT

Magnetic superstar Elizabeth Taylor waits for tea to be served by Mia Farrow in the John Heyman/Norman Priggen production *Secret Ceremony*, directed by Joseph Losey

turned into reality. EMI (Electrical and Musical Industries), one of Britain's biggest and most influential conglomerates, purchased the remaining Warner stake in the Associated British Picture Corporation in 1968 and saw the further full ownership of that company as a natural and progressive extension of their industry hardware business. After a short fierce industry battle they acquired controlling interests in A.B.P.C. in February, 1969.

With the new take-over Sir Philip Warter, Robert Clark and C.J. Latta were to go their separate ways and at the shareholders' meeting for the year ending the 30th June 1969, Sir Joseph Lockwood, EMI's chief executive (who had quietly and successfully manoeuvred the company towards its peak position over the years) announced the new board of directors. It was an impressive roll call.

John Read who had been EMI Group Managing Director, was now appointed Chief Executive of EMI. Bernard Delfont (later Lord Delfont) was appointed Chairman and Chief Executive of A.B.P.C. He was in turn to appoint Nat Cohen,

Roger Moore steps off the set of *The Man Who Haunted Himself* to visit Peter Sellers and Sinead Cusack on the nearby set of *Hoffman*

Managing Director of Anglo-Amalgamated and Leslie Grade, Managing Director of the Grade Organisation, to the A.B.P.C. board; and create a new Head of Production and Managing Director of Elstree Studios, Bryan Forbes.

Forbes had started in the industry as an actor, become a screen writer of distinction and finally a film director of merit, and he approached his new position with a complete faith in the British film industry and a bubbling enthusiasm for Elstree. He announced an ambitious star-studded production programme and set to work immediately.

His first two films were *The Man Who Haunted Himself*, produced by Michael Relph and directed by Basil Dearden, with Roger Moore starring in this psychological mystery of a man whose double image takes possession after a near fatal car crash; and *Hoffman*, with the inimitable Peter Sellers in a yarn about the amorous adventures of a timid bachelor. By the time Forbes's third production *And Soon the Darkness*, produced by Albert Fennell and Brian Clemens, was taking the floor, the old Porridge Factory had accepted the fact that the former B.I.P./A.B.P.C. days were over. For while EMI had been exemplary in their solicitude for the studio staff, the change had, understandably, been difficult for some of the old hands to accept.

EMI had started its reign with a bold and courageous production programme – and an eye to yet further expansion. They did not have to look very far. Down the road, the M.G.M. studios (the old Amalgamated Studios that John Maxwell had wanted to acquire thirty years earlier) were beginning to feel the pinch from the withdrawal of international production finance, television competition – and the cut-back of their own parent company in the States.

Chapter 7

The Seventies: Battle for Survival

Thorn-EMI Elstree Studios, Borehamwood, Hertfordshire

THE M.G.M.-British studios, Elstree (Borehamwood) had always had the aura of glamour, razzmatazz and luxury that typified a powerful, legendary American film company. Not for them the early battles of the twenties onwards, for survival and prominence, like the old Porridge Factory, now the EMI studios, though their parent company in the States had carved themselves a huge hunk of film history over the decades. But for their new offspring setting up their first Elstree production in 1948/49, the proud parents wanted to bestow all the advantages of a noble film birthright that they could muster – and they did. While Britain was still reeling from the aftermath of war in the forties, M.G.M. studios opened their opulent doors with a fanfare of

trumpets and a spilling of coffers that gladdened the hearts of the British Film Industry and the Chancellor of the Exchequer alike.

From their first major production in 1949 of George Cukor's *Edward My Son*, starring Spencer Tracy as a callous millionaire and Deborah Kerr as his slighted, alcoholic spouse, they proceeded through the fifties and the sixties to produce films that were to attract American and British stars to the British Hollywood and enthusiastic queues at the cinemas.

They were to include *The Miniver Story*, with the ever popular Greer Garson, Walter Pidgeon and John Hodiak; smash hit *Ivanhoe* with fair damsels in distress Elizabeth Taylor and Joan Fontaine being rescued by the valiant Robert Taylor; *Mog-*

143

Touching performances from Nanette Newman and Malcolm McDowell in *The Raging Moon*, produced by Bruce Cohn Curtis and directed by Bryan Forbes

for it was to mean that there would be just one surviving studio at Elstree. The blow was to be somewhat softened though, in April 1970 by a joint statement from Mr John Read (later Sir John), chief executive of EMI and Mr James T. Aubrey Junior, president of M.G.M., to the effect that although M.G.M. was to close its own studios, it would immediately take advantage of the EMI Elstree studio facilities and form a joint association with EMI. The Old Porridge Factory was to be re-christened EMI–M.G.M. Elstree Studios Ltd, in return for which M.G.M. would guarantee an annual subsidy of £175,000.

'We have attempted to present talent at all levels and we are prepared to be judged on the ultimate results,' was the courageous slogan penned by Bryan Forbes on the studio envelopes and if that meant variety, then variety was about to be given. Vampires, wheelchairs, Victorian children, thugs, misers and a transplanted penis, were among the offerings of the 1970 Elstree production schedule

ambo (a remake of the 1932 film *Red Dust*) directed by master veteran John Ford, with the cool and lovely Grace Kelly and beautiful, sultry Ava Gardner, making life very difficult for Clark Gable and Donald Sinden; and the charming story of *The Yellow Rolls Royce* and its successive owners, written by Terence Rattigan and starring Shirley MacLaine, Omar Sharif, Rex Harrison, Edmund Purdom, Ingrid Bergman and George C. Scott. In 1968, Stanley Kubrick's *2001: A Space Odyssey*, a science fiction saga, was made in deep secrecy and a year later M.G.M.'s *Goodbye Mr Chips* took to the floor with Peter O'Toole and Petula Clark doing a fine job of turning the 1939 weepie into a 1969 musical.

With an impressive twenty-year production record to their credit, it was not surprising that take-over bids should be in the air and when sadly in 1970, the news broke of considerable losses and a massive withdrawal of American investment, it became clear that the studios were no longer economically viable and that closure was imminent.

The news was yet another hard blow for the film industry and the British Hollywood in particular.

and it would be difficult to visualise a more varied programme than that.

The vampires were in fact two Hammer offerings. *The Vampire Lovers* should perhaps have been retitled Them Femme Fatale Fangs, seeing that it was the tale of a lesbian vampire on the lookout for unsuspecting maidenforms, but good old *Lust for a Vampire* stuck to the rule book and gave the time-honoured prescription of a nineteenth century castle, a devastating blonde in a tight bodice, an absent-minded (one might say positively dim) young professor and a somewhat overdone stake: providing an absolute feast for the many House of Hammer fans.

The wheelchairs and the Victorian children were in fact part of the Bryan Forbes/EMI production programme. *The Raging Moon*, starring Nanette Newman and Malcolm McDowell and directed by Forbes, was the story of a cripple and a polio victim, who, confined to wheelchairs, meet in hospital, spark each other back to life and fall in love. *The Railway Children*, based on the novel by E. Nesbit and directed by Lionel Jeffries with loving care, was to become one of our most successful and best loved children's features.

In *Dulcima*, Sir John Mills played the lecherous old miser whose attentions are turned down by the local farmer's daughter (Carol White) until she realises that he is far from being the penniless recluse that he pretends to be. While last, but by no means least, the Betty Box production of *Percy* starred Hywel Bennett in a comedy about a man trying to find the donor of his transplanted penis.

In spite of the reduced cinema attendances, due in the main to the growing television audiences and a decline in British film production, which in turn was due in large part to the declining volume of financial support from the American majors, who were encountering cash-flow problems of their own, EMI–M.G.M. took the bit between their teeth and countered with considerable indigenous financing and the setting up of a substantial further production.

While Roy Simpson was preparing his children's television series *The Double Deckers*, other crews were becoming accustomed to passing the time of day with Mrs Tiggy-Winkle, Jemima Puddle-Duck,

ABOVE
Barbara Jefford and Mike Raven obviously get on like a house of fire in the 1970 Hammer horror movie *Lust for a Vampire*

LEFT
The attentions of a lecherous miser (John Mills) are rejected by the farmer's daughter (Carol White) until she realises that he is not as penniless as he pretends in *Dulcima*, based on a story by H. E. Bates

145

Sir Frederick Ashton rehearsing members of the Royal
Ballet for *Tales of Beatrix Potter*

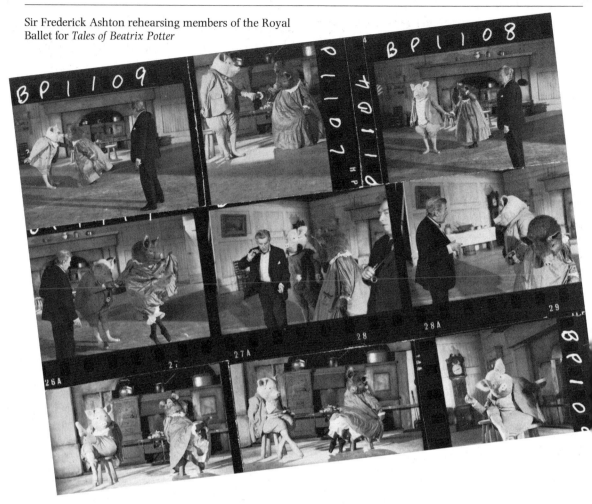

Mrs Tittlemouse and sundry friends. With flair and imagination, producers John Brabourne (Lord Brabourne) and Richard Goodwin had decided to film *The Tales of Beatrix Potter*, with Sir Frederick Ashton and members of the Royal Ballet performing versions of some of the stories of this much loved classic, in animal costume. Their hunch was to pay off, for the film won a number of awards and acclaim from the critics; and if because of its success, Jeremy Fisher was to become Jeremie Pêche à la Ligne and Squirrel Nutkin was to become known as Eichhornchen Nusskern on their travels, it only added to the film's international reputation.

With such a marvellous start to the seventies, the studios were booming, and all nine sound stages were busy with big feature and television series. The 350-strong department of carpenters, plasterers, painters, riggers and stage-hands was sometimes called upon to build as many as fifteen different sets at a time; and to conjure up structural miracles from wood, canvas, plaster, fibre glass, sponge rubber and plastic materials, for such things as house interiors and furniture, twelve times their actual size for *The Tales of Beatrix Potter*, or a Roman forum and slave market for *Up Pompeii*. This featured the hugely popular, pursed lipped comedian Frankie Howerd cavorting in good orgy fashion to the background music of Carl Davis.

There was to be something of a leap, though, from Pompeii to Newcastle-upon-Tyne, for Michael Klinger's production of *Get Carter*, based at Elstree. Sleepy-eyed heart-throb Michael Caine was to turn in a compelling performance as a sardonic crook out to avenge his brother's gang warfare death, with Ian Hendry, Britt Ekland and actor/writer John Osborne in supporting roles. But for true terror one had only to take two fearful footsteps to the adjoining set. There *The Abominable*

Vincent Price as *The Abominable Dr Phibes*. A complicated tale of horror and revenge, it kept the Elstree special effects team busy creating items such as a macabre shrine and a clockwork pop group

ABOVE
Comedian Frankie Howerd dampens the enthusiasm of a hardy centurion in *Up Pompeii*

RIGHT
Elstree's hot line: Michael Caine plays a sardonic crook out to avenge his brother's death in *Get Carter*

147

Dr Phibes, alias the incomparable Vincent Price, was making a spectacle of himself in a flowing red cape, in a complicated tale of horror about a mad, disfigured doctor, who visits the nine curses of Egypt on the doctors who he feels were responsible for the death of his wife. Nightmares like this, though, were all in a day's work for the Elstree backroom boys who, without turning a hair on

LEFT
Lovely Julie Christie in *The Go-Between*

BELOW
Grand Prix winner at Cannes 1971 was the John Heyman/Norman Priggen production *The Go-Between*. In this scene Marian (Julie Christie) watches her lover Ted (Alan Bates) being applauded after a good innings by spectators including her fiance Hugh (Edward Fox)

end, produced a splendidly baroque haunted ball-room in horrendous tones of pink and mauve, a glowing demonic electric organ which descended Reg Dixon style into a macabre shrine, and a clockwork pop group of the period, which was supposed to keep in tune with Dr Phibes's ghostly organ accompaniment. Veteran Hollywood actor Joseph Cotten, was also in there . . . . somewhere.

With no hint as yet of management changes, but ringing the feature changes yet again, EMI-M.G.M. were to announce with understandable pride their production of *The Go-Between*, an Edwardian romance by L.P. Hartley. If ever a film was able to capture England at the turn of the century, with its class distinction, social graces and mellow country-side (superbly photographed by Geoffrey Fisher), it must surely have been this one. Julie Christie, Alan Bates, Edward Fox, Margaret Leighton and Sir

Michael Redgrave starred in this delicately directed Joseph Losey film, from a screenplay by Harold Pinter. It went on to win the Grand Prix at Cannes in 1971.

In March 1971, Elstree again hit the headlines with the news that Bryan Forbes was to relinquish his responsibilities as head of production and managing director of EMI–M.G.M. Elstree studios. An announcement from the board stated that in a shorter time than was thought possible, Forbes had brilliantly executed the two main services for which he had been engaged: to bring to life the EMI Studios at Elstree and to make them an efficient and productive film-making unit. Ian Scott, a chartered accountant and a director of Associated British Productions in 1969, who had transferred to Elstree in 1962 from Associated British-Pathe, was appointed as the new managing director of the studios. An old colleague, also making the trade headlines at that time, was fellow Scot Andrew Mitchell. He had joined A.B.P.C. in 1955 and been associate producer on a number of Elstree films, including the Cliff Richard successes *The Young Ones, Summer Holiday* and *Wonderful Life*. Now he had been appointed managing director of Leslie Grade Films Ltd.

Changes or no, the show must go on, and what better offering than Ken Russell's *The Boy Friend*, based on the Sandy Wilson twenties musical. A show within a show, it drew delightful performances from Twiggy and Christopher Gable with a tremendous supporting cast, who gave their all to such lovely old numbers as *I Could Be Happy With You, You Are My Lucky Star* and *A Room In Bloomsbury*.

With the Cannes Grand Prix for *The Go-Between* in their pockets, Bernard Delfont (later Lord Delfont) and Nat Cohen decided on one of their most lavish and ambitious projects to date – a new film version of *Henry VIII and his Six Wives*. Considering old Henry was married to his first wife Catherine of Aragon for over twenty years, it certainly took him some time to officially go off the rails, but once he had made the first leap, there appeared to be no holding him. Divorced, Beheaded, Died, Divorced, Beheaded, Survived, were to be the fates of his six brides, who in the film were played by Frances

Anne Boleyn (Charlotte Rampling) bids for a king (Keith Michell) and wins in *Henry VIII and his Six Wives*

Twiggy and Christopher Gable in *The Boy Friend*

Cuka, Charlotte Rampling, Jane Asher, Jenny Bos, Lynne Frederick and Barbara Leigh-Hunt, to Keith Michell's Henry. Outstanding sets and costumes helped to make this film, produced by Mark Shivas and Roy Baird and directed by Waris Hussein, a sure winner.

It would have taken more than a few beheadings, though, to frighten off Sir James Carreras's House of Hammer. Such child's play was not for them and they continued to fill the cinemas with their staple diet of Draculas, obsessed barons, family curses and the usual dosage of blood and thunder. From time to time, though, they would relieve the tension somewhat and just settle for a modern, nerve-tingling thriller like *Fear in the Night* with Peter Cushing and Joan Collins.

With the withdrawal of top American investment in the early seventies, it also meant that the British Hollywood was to see less of the American stars and EMI certainly went out of its way to boost an indigenous film industry in every respect and give British stars, technicians, producers and writers a chance to shine. With important success like *The Railway Children*, *The Go-Between*, and *Henry VIII and his Six Wives*, they had made an outstanding start with their film division acquisition.

Elstree's two British comics for the seventies were to be Reg Varney and Frankie Howerd. Howerd had already starred in *Up Pompeii*, which was followed with a medieval romp called *Up the Chastity Belt*. With a plot centred around this device and characters dubbed Lurkalot, Sir Coward de Custard and Chopper the Woodman – all meeting regularly at the Crusaders' Arms, instead of taking them up – students of G.M. Trevelyan were not in any serious danger of being tricked out of their homework heritage. In fact, Frankie as King Richard dallying with the dusky Scheherazade (Eartha Kitt), probably gave a whole new meaning to the term Lionhearted. On the other hand, television favourite Reg Varney was to go in for more modern humour, with *On the Buses*, *Mutiny on the Buses* and a holiday camp skit, produced by Johnny Goodman and Andrew Mitchell, called *The Best Pair of Legs in the Business*.

It must have been gratifying to EMI's chief executive John Read to note the accruing profits and prizes that the company had continued to gain. *Baxter*, with Patricia Neal, Jean-Pierre Cassel and Lynn Carlin, was to win an award at the Norwegian Film Festival, while the science fiction feature *The Final Programme* with Jon Finch and Jenny Runacre was to pick up a special prize at the 'Festival International d'Avoriaz du Film'. To add to these fillips news came that magnetic star Elizabeth Taylor would shortly be arriving to make *Night Watch* with Laurence Harvey and Billie Whitelaw. Accompanying the news was a request for Miss Taylor's own kitchen and special chef at the studio. A compromise was reached and the cast took to the floor for this psychological thriller.

By the end of 1972, in spite of the studio's successes, U.K. box office takings were beginning to nose dive with a vengeance and independent producers were beginning to feel the pinch. There were to be three brave productions, though. Henrik Ibsen's *A Doll's House* starred Claire Bloom, Anthony Hopkins, Dame Edith Evans and Sir Ralph Richardson. Stanley Donen's *The Little Prince*, with lyrics and music by Alan Jay Lerner and Frederick Loewe, told the story of a prince who leaves his planet to learn about life on earth and who encounters some strange beings, like dancer/choreographer Bob Fosse as a snake in the grass. Third was another Cliff Richard special from producer Kenneth Harper called *Take Me High*. Cliff, the teenage idol, was by now an incredibly youthful thirty-three-year-old and yet again was to have the kids jumping in the aisles in his role of a young, swinging, financial tycoon who falls for the charms of lovely Debbie Watling.

But sadly, box office returns continued to dive. Towards the end of 1973 British studios were beginning to lose money and Elstree was no exception. An even bigger blow was the news that M.G.M. in the States was withdrawing from motion picture distribution and also drastically cutting back on its film production, which in turn was to mean the withdrawal of M.G.M.'s £175,000 annual participation in the EMI Elstree studio.

An announcement from M.G.M.'s president James Aubrey declared, 'We can no longer continue to operate in a manner and scope designed years ago when motion pictures were the principal form of entertainment. The bottom has fallen out of the market.'

'This could be the end of the line for Elstree' were the trade headlines – and they were so right.

In August of 1973, Ian Scott left the studios to join Thames Television and Andrew Mitchell, who already had a long association with the studios as well as many years of practical film making experience, was appointed managing director of Elstree studios. Had he known it, he could not have taken up his appointment at a more crucial time in the studios' history.

EMI's chief executive, John Read, had the unpleasant duty of laying it on the line for the industry and studios alike by stating the facts. 'The films we make on our own cannot possibly support the entire studio operation,' he said. 'There have to be other films from outside producers and companies to make the studio viable. This is a severe problem and is made even worse by the withdrawal of M.G.M.'

Claire Bloom and Anthony Hopkins in a scene from *A Doll's House*, the 1972 version of the Ibsen play

Faye Dunaway headed a star cast in *Voyage of the Damned*, an I.T.C. Entertainment production

By November 1973, the permanent studio staff of 479 had been cut to 256 and the closure of the old Porridge Factory seemed imminent. And yet . . . and yet . . . it just would not give up the ghost. Whether that ghost was the studios' founder Scottish John Maxwell, whose protégé was the Scottish Robert Clark, whose protégé in turn was the Scottish Andrew Mitchell, we shall never know. But one thing we do know for certain, those who stayed shared Mitchell's almost crusading zeal to keep the studios open and against all odds, they managed to do just that.

For their part EMI decided to make their most ambitious film ever, with a galaxy of international stars. It was Agatha Christie's *Murder on the Orient Express* and starred Albert Finney, Ingrid Bergman, Sean Connery, Lauren Bacall, Sir John Gielgud, Jean-Pierre Cassel, Richard Widmark, Wendy Hiller and many more. Produced by John

Brabourne and Richard Goodwin and directed by Sidney Lumet, it was to be an enormous success at the box office as well as receiving six Oscar nominations (which included Geoffrey Unsworth's cinematography and Tony Walton's costume designs).

Every hand-picked star in the cast gave an individual and memorable performance. Even the famous Belgian detective Hercule Poirot (Albert Finney) conceded that the two hours he had spent in the make-up chair every morning to acquire a false nose, hair dye, puffed cheeks and body padding, for a twenty-year age gap and character change, were worth every moment.

Confessions of a Window Cleaner was a complete contrast. At first glance it would seem to be yet another domestic piece, but in fact there were to be a series of *Confessions* films and while none of them could be termed blockbusters, they provided excellent returns for their producers and essential life blood for the ailing studio. They were produced by Greg Smith, a young man who, like David Puttnam, through dint of effort and a refusal to take no for an answer, managed to raise film capital and get productions off the ground. Director of the film Val Guest had known the studios from the early B.I.P. days. He had started as a pressman, gone on to become a screenwriter and then a director, with clear recollections of Hitchcock's practical jokes. Having lent Hitch a fiver on one occasion, he had been less than enchanted to receive it back in the form of a sackful of ha'pennies. He had reciprocated by collecting a huge bag of old keys, which he then had dropped all over London by chums, on buses, on trains, and in theatres. Each key had been labelled with Hitchcock's name and address, complete with the message, 'If returned there will be an award of £5.00.' A week later an enraged Hitch had burst into his office with 'How many of those bloody keys did you leave about for God's sake?'

The Maids, played by Glenda Jackson and Susannah York, evolved a sadistic ritual to speed the demise of their employer, but failed to go through with it. A Robert Enders and Bernard Weitzman production, with the usual wizardry from the camera of Douglas Slocombe. Two further prestigious offerings were to come from Ely Landau: *Galileo*, a beautifully observed film about

RIGHT
Poster for *Murder on the Orient Express*, 1974

FINNEY

BALSAM

BISSET

CONNERY

HILLER

REDGRAVE

WIDMARK

BACALL

BERGMAN

CASSEL

GIELGUD

PERKINS

ROBERTS

YORK

NAT COHEN PRESENTS FOR EMI FILM DISTRIBUTORS LTD.
A JOHN BRABOURNE-RICHARD GOODWIN PRODUCTION

AGATHA CHRISTIE'S

MURDER
ON
THE
ORIENT EXPRESS

ALBERT FINNEY · LAUREN BACALL
MARTIN BALSAM · INGRID BERGMAN · JACQUELINE BISSET
JEAN-PIERRE CASSEL · SEAN CONNERY · JOHN GIELGUD
WENDY HILLER · ANTHONY PERKINS · VANESSA REDGRAVE
RACHEL ROBERTS · RICHARD WIDMARK · MICHAEL YORK
WITH COLIN BLAKELY · GEORGE COULOURIS · DENIS QUILLEY
MUSIC COMPOSED BY RICHARD RODNEY BENNETT · SCREENPLAY BY PAUL DEHN
PRODUCED BY JOHN BRABOURNE & RICHARD GOODWIN · DIRECTED BY SIDNEY LUMET
RELEASED BY EMI FILM DISTRIBUTORS LTD. · TECHNICOLOR

EMI

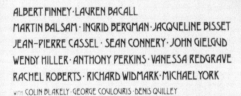

the great man with excellent performances from Topol, Edward Fox, Tom Conti, Sir John Gielgud and Margaret Leighton; and *In Celebration*, the event being the reunion of three miner's sons, who meet on their father's fortieth wedding anniversary; the film was produced by Otto Plaschkes and directed by Lindsay Anderson.

Almost sixty years in the business and looking younger by the minute, the incredible cinematographer Freddie Young was back on the Elstree floor for *Great Expectations*. Freddie's association with the studio went right back to the British and Dominions days, with Anna Neagle, Jack Buchanan and Herbert Wilcox, to whom he had been under contract from 1928 to 1939. But even with three Oscars on his bookcase – for *Lawrence of Arabia, Dr Zhivago* and *Ryan's Daughter* – he seemed delighted to be back at the old Porridge Factory where his career had taken wings. James Mason, Michael York and Sarah Miles were to provide marvellous material for his camera.

Three British lovelies were to bring the studios into the mid seventies. Joan Collins enticing *Alfie Darling* (Alan Price) to a candlelit dinner for two . . . plus; and Vanessa Redgrave and Susan George in *Out of Season*, also starring Cliff Robertson and directed by Alan Bridges, a film which spelt out the relationship between a mother and daughter who receive a visitor from the past, during their winter isolation in a seaside guest house.

Yes, the studios had picked themselves up in an incredible fashion, but the battle for survival was not over. Elstree, along with its fellow studios, was still losing money and in February 1975, EMI sadly announced that six of the nine stages would be closed with 213 redundancies leaving a skeleton staff of forty-eight. That, said a great number of film folk, is certainly that, and started to fly the flags at half mast.

It was to be a premature burial. Six months later the EMI studios were still alive, well and living at Elstree, and Andrew Mitchell was able to boast one of the 'finest facilities studios' in Europe. What the studio had done was to streamline its old form, with all equipment intact, and to modernise for the future. The new facilities studio was to mean total freedom for the independent producer, who could hire whom and what he wanted for any given period, including stages, offices, equipment, workshops, transport and expertise. The studio was now also free from the massive overheads of former days. Flying the flag even further, EMI's

director of overseas distribution Michael Bromhead took off on a massive sales drive and Nat Cohen, chairman and chief executive of EMI Film Distributors announced that a number of films were to be made at Elstree Studios. The long haul back was under way.

Not to be outdone, Lord Grade gave the British film industry in general, and Elstree in particular, something to cheer about. *The Voyage of the Damned*, with a £3,000,000 budget, took to stage three, with a cast list that looked as if a cluster of diamonds had been scattered on to a black velvet drape. Star carats Faye Dunaway, Max von Sydow, Orson Welles, Julie Harris, James Mason, Janet Suzman, Jose Ferrer and many more came together for this film based on a true incident: that of 937 German Jews boarding a luxury cruise ship in 1939 to sail to Cuba. What they did not know, was that the Nazis would put pressure on Cuba to refuse landing permission and thus have them sent back to Germany and certain death.

This was to be followed by the Robert Enders production of *Hedda*, for which Glenda Jackson was to receive an Oscar, and Aida Young's *The Likely Lads*, a spin off from the very popular television show.

One thing had been conspicuous by its absence over the last few years – the sadly missed American presence in the British Hollywood. But in 1976, although still facing their own film legislative problems, the Americans started to drift back to Elstree and after the recent dark years, it was good to welcome old friends back. United Artists were to invest in *Valentino*, with Rudolf Nureyev in the name part, showing that he could be an actor of depth as well as a magnificent dancer. Leslie Caron and Felicity Kendal were also to star in this film, which was to have Stanley Black as its musical director. Black had a very long association with the studios and had worked on more than a hundred motion pictures; he also had a tremendous admiration for the director Ken Russell, whose own knowledge of music was considerable.

Certainly Andrew Mitchell's new look studios were beginning to flourish, and Twentieth Century Fox decided on two Elstree productions. The first

RIGHT
Released in 1977 and directed by Ken Russell, *Valentino* proved that Rudolf Nureyev, in the name part, was an excellent actor as well as a magnificent dancer. He is seen here with Michelle Phillips

With extraordinary insight, Fred Zinnemann chose two leading ladies for his film *Julia* who must surely have represented the British Hollywood as no other two stars had done before them. Jane Fonda (left) and Venessa Redgrave

was to be *Julia* based on Lillian Hellman's book *Pentimento*, founded on a schoolgirl friendship in her own life and a later dramatic development. With extraordinary insight that remarkable director Fred Zinnemann chose two ladies who must surely have represented the British Hollywood, as perhaps no other two stars had done before them, in any given era. Jane Fonda, born in New York, the daughter of star father, Henry Fonda, with a string of movie successes to her credit, including *Barbarella* and *Klute*. In the other corner, Vanessa Redgrave, born in London, daughter of distinguished actor Sir Michael Redgrave, and already an acclaimed star with such films as *Camelot*, *Isadora* and *Mary Queen of Scots* behind her.

The second Twentieth Century release was to be

the biggest blockbuster that the studios had ever seen. Produced by Gary Kurtz and directed by George Lucas, it was called *Star Wars*. With joint American and British expertise it went on to win four Oscars for Best Sound, Best Visual Effects, Best Costume Design and Best Art Direction, and by December 1980 it had grossed $510,000,000 world wide.

The British Hollywood positively hummed over this one with an eighteen-week (principal photography) shoot. A space era, inter-planetary adventure, with literally black and white baddies and goodies, outstanding special effects and a James Bond flavour all rolled into one. It starred Carrie Fisher, Mark Hamill, Harrison Ford, Sir Alec Guinness and two delightful robots who were to steal not a little of the starlight. See Threepio (C3PO) was played by Anthony Daniels and Artoo-Detoo (R2-D2) by Kenny Baker.

In 1976 EMI decided on yet another acquisition in a swift and dramatic move that took the industry by surprise. A British independent company, British Lion Films, was bought in August of that year and some months later former British Lion chiefs Barry Spikings and Michael Deeley were confirmed as joint managing directors of the newly titled EMI Films Ltd. Meanwhile the studios were intent on keeping the television as well as feature fans happy, by turning the popular television series *Are You Being Served?* into a full length feature; while on a sister stage I.T.C.'s *Return of the Saint* now starred Ian Ogilvy, who had succeeded Roger Moore in the part.

In 1977 British cinemas were again facing a massive shut-down and cinemas and the trade associations alike were crying out for Eady Levy relief – some form of self-help legislation – and better remuneration and safeguards for films shown on television. But the government's Annan report was to bring groans of despair from any film industry association hoping that television would be statutorily bound to plough back some of its profits into the film industry. Kenneth Maidment, president of the Film Producers' Association, was

forced to the sombre comment 'that there is nothing in Annan which gives us encouragement for our immediate future'; Alan Sapper, general secretary of the A.C.T.T., was to describe it as a 'dog's breakfast', while Hugh Orr, president of the Association of Independent Cinemas, was to state that 'the whole thing is completely out of touch with modern thinking about a viable operation in the financial state that we are in.' It was unusual to see the entire industry in such harmony.

But as always, in a bout of depression, show business was to provide escapism and glamour to blow the blues away; this time with a story based on the life of Aristotle Onassis and Jacqueline Kennedy (though this was much denied at the time). Director J. Lee-Thompson was to provide

Are You Being Served?, the popular TV series, was turned into a full-length feature in 1977. Directed by Bob Kellett and produced by Andrew Mitchell, it starred Mollie Sugden, John Inman, Frank Thornton and Trevor Bannister

ABOVE
Oscar-winning blockbuster *Star Wars*, the space era inter-planetary adventure, produced by Gary Kurtz in 1977 and directed by George Lucas. Seen here are Carrie Fisher, Harrison Ford, Mark Hamill and friend

RIGHT
Even the lights starred: Alec Guinness prepares for a scene in *Star Wars*. British expertise was not confined to acting and special effects in the making of the film. For the location shots in Tunisia, Thorn Lighting's CSI lamps were used. Unique to Thorn, the main advantage of this light source is its high light output which gives very powerful beams from small, easily rigged, lightweight equipment. Still in sparkling form, the Thorn CSI lamp has an up-dated sister model, used at the Royal Wedding in 1981

160

yachts, riches, sleek Jacqueline Bisset and the electric Anthony Quinn in *The Greek Tycoon*. And just to keep the hearts a-flutter, another romance was being made at the studios, this time with Lesley-Anne Down as a Red Cross nurse, Harrison Ford as a bomber pilot and Christopher Plummer as the blitzed husband, in London's war-torn *Hanover Street*, produced by Paul Lazarus III.

While EMI was to merge its distribution arm with Columbia–Warner in 1978, the studios were to have further welcome production news. Stanley Kubrick's *The Shining* was to take the floor after months of pre-production work and EMI were to build an enormous silent stage on the back lot for the *Star Wars 2* film, *The Empire Strikes Back*, to commence the following year. At a calculated minimum cost of six hundred thousand pounds, it came as a welcome boost to the industry.

As the shaky seventies drew to a close, it was evident that the studio had pulled itself up by its very gut strings, from near disaster, and was going to survive. It could never again be the huge family concern, with seepages, gags, anecdotes and padding. It could not afford to be. But in its place was a streamlined, modernised, very personalised studio, with a great sense of pride in its achievements. Old timers like John Wilcox and Freddie Young working on *Stevie* must have noted the changes. But even in this new finery, the old Elstree studios were not always on their best behaviour. There was, for example, the bogus prince who got himself whisked down to the studios to discuss a million dollar

RIGHT
Stars Wars 2 – The Empire Strikes Back: bossy C3PO (Anthony Daniels) and his chubby little friend R2-D2 (Kenny Baker)

BELOW
Director J. Lee-Thompson was to provide yachts, riches, sleek Jacqueline Bisset and Anthony Quinn in *The Greek Tycoon*

Mona Washbourne and Glenda Jackson
in *Stevie*. Directed by Robert Enders and written by
Hugh Whitemore, it was based on the life of poetess
Stevie Smith

And in spite of television, or perhaps because of it, (and certainly the medium had contributed much to the studios' 'bread and butter'), the blockbusters were still there. *The Empire Strikes Back* was now under way on the completed silent stage, with producers Gary Kurtz and George Lucas and director Irvin Kershner now feeling very much at home in their Elstree galaxy.

In November 1979, Elstree Studios were to have another change within the parent company. Thorn, the British electrical giant headed by Sir Richard Cave, made a £169,000,000 bid for EMI and with the amalgamation came the name change to Thorn EMI. Thorn's involvement with Elstree studios has resulted in a modernisation programme which today includes twenty-seven new cutting rooms, two new property stores and a new special effects building, plus modernisation in the post-production area including automatic dialogue replacement.

Yes, it was still business as usual at the old Porridge Factory and just to make that point quite clear, Evelyn Laye, the enchanting British musical comedy star of the twenties and thirties, was back at the studios to make the *Never Never Land* with Petula Clark and Cathleen Nesbitt.

And should there have been lingering doubts in anyone's mind, cables arrived from Steven Spielberg in the States to confirm that he would be commencing principal photography on *Raiders of the Lost Ark*, in 1980 – at Elstree, the British Hollywood.

deal, before being whisked back into police custody. There was the fire that swept through *The Shining* set on stage three in 1979, causing damage at an estimated one and quarter million pounds, certainly reminding Wilcox of the fire that caused his own father, Herbert, to leave the studios way back in the thirties.

Chapter 8
The Way Ahead

'As I write this report, we are surrounded by more new legislation than ever before, and I suspect that we will be seeing a lot more in the future. Indeed, it would not be unfair to say that the industry is going through a revolution as it prepares itself for the second half of the decade.'

Kenneth L. Maidment, President of The British Film and Television Producers' Association, 1982.

'The time has come for the Government and the House to look at the whole cinema industry. The legislation goes back to the 1927 statute, when Al Jolson appeared in the first talking film, The Jazz Singer. *It does not take proper account of the arrival of cable, satellite, video and television.'*

Iain Sproat, Under-Secretary of State for Trade, 1982

THE CHARAGRAPH; TO BRIGHTEN THE HOMEWARD JOURNEY AFTER DARK.

BOTH these statements describe the state of the current film industry in a nutshell, and the recent Hunt report on British cable television, published in October 1982, adds further complications to the already complex situation.

But just as there have always been complications in our British film industry – the advent of sound, for example – so there will always be opportunities for anyone willing to accept the challenge of the future. Our present day film technology is due in no small measure to the dedication and determination of our early film pioneers. The last remaining studios at Elstree took up the gauntlet in 1927 and today are still continuing their dogged path into the future.

Now the Thorn–EMI Studios, the 'old Porridge Factory', while proud of their achievements, are still aware of industry problems. Nevertheless the studios invest and prepare for the shape of things to come. In 1980, Peter Laister, managing director of Thorn EMI took on 'overall responsibility for the company's entertainment group', and emphasised the company's commitment to the production and marketing of motion pictures throughout the world. Since then the studios have continued their effective open facilities format and attracted old and new friends, British and American producers, to its complex.

Producer George ('Star Wars') Lucas and director Steven Spielberg arrived with their stars, Harrison Ford and Karen Allen, to occupy five of

ABOVE
Anne Archer, Ryan O'Neal and Omar Sharif in a romantic comedy-thriller *Green Ice*, an I.T.C. Entertainment production

LEFT
Harrison Ford in the exciting adventure *Raiders of the Lost Ark*, produced by George Lucas and directed by Steven Spielberg

the studios' sound stages for a ten month shooting period for the blockbuster *Raiders of the Lost Ark*. A marvellous adventure set in the thirties, concerning lost treasure, sinister agents, wonderful stunts and a handsome hero, the film appealed to all ages. So did *The Great Muppet Caper*, which had that volatile star of stage and screen, Miss Piggy — supremely handled by Jim Henson, Frank Oz and David Lazer.

Also booked in at the beginning of the eighties

were *The Final Conflict* with Rossano Brazzi, and *Green Ice*, a romantic comedy/thriller with Ryan O'Neal, Anne Archer and Omar Sharif, produced by Jack Wiener and directed by Anthony Simmons. In no time at all George Lucas was back for the *Return Of The Jedi* (scheduled for a 1983 release) with his *Star Wars* team. *The Monster Club*, *George and Mildred*, *Venom*, *Dark Crystal*, a television version of *Oliver Twist* and *The Shillingbury Tales* also went into production.

Perhaps it should fall to Val Guest, director of *The Shillingbury Tales* and associated with Elstree over many years, to tell the oldest studio anecdote of all. Anyone who has worked at Elstree knows the story well, but Guest declares that he was there when it

OVERLEAF
Temperamental star of stage and screen Miss Piggy being coaxed into action by Kermit the frog in *The Great Muppet Caper*, an I.T.C. Entertainment production

happened. The legendary Joe Grossman, the Cockney studio manager in the thirties, was escorting
the King of Greece on a tour of the studios. With his
nervous twitch working overtime and having
donned his best uniform for the occasion (he was
also head of the studio fire brigade), he commenced
his official patter thus: 'In this film, your Majesty,
we are using all the 'abitats of a cafe – the camera is
put inside that box cos we don't want to 'ear
anything, and the thing up there on a pole is a
boom and the sound goes through the air . . . . .
but I h'expect this is all Greek to you . . .'

The Monty Python team on the backlot of
Thorn-EMI Elstree Studios during the
filming of *Monty Pythons The Meaning of Life*,
produced by John Goldstone and directed by
Terry Jones. Left to right, Graham
Chapman, Terry Jones, Michael Palin, Terry
Gilliam, John Cleese and Eric Idle

On set of *Reilly*, a twelve-part spy thriller series made
by Thames Television's subsidiary Euston Films. Sam
Neill plays the role of Sidney Reilly, based on the life of
a man acknowledged by many to have been the
greatest of all espionage agents

Dear Joe Grossman would certainly have approved of his beloved studios today, although he would have been in for a few surprises. Although his house is still exactly as it was in his day (it is now used for visiting production teams), and the 'props' and stills library are housed in the last remaining part of the original building, his official commentary would have had to have been enormously up-dated, along these lines.

The studio is fully equipped to service all types of production in 35mm and 16mm photography. Comprising nine stages, including the largest purpose-built stage in Europe and three with television lighting grids, there are on site Front Projection and Photographic Effects services and comprehensive modern post production facilities for 35mm and 16mm productions, including high speed A.D.R. There are also twenty-seven new cutting rooms and Film and Sound Library Services. Additional amenities include a restaurant, a cafeteria and a bar.

As 1982 draws to a close, with Brian North as chief executive of Thorn-EMI Films, the Thorn-EMI Elstree studios are working to full capacity with productions that include *Reilly*, a television series produced by Chris Burt, Verity Lambert, now di-

Sean Connery plays
Secret Agent 007 James
Bond in *Never Say Never
Again*, produced by Jack
Schwartzman and
directed by Irvin
Kerschner for Woodcote
Productions Ltd/Warner
Brothers

rector of production for Thorn-EMI Films Ltd, and Johnny Goodman for Euston Films, starring Sam Neill, Leo McKern and Jeananne Crowley; *Monty Python's The Meaning of Life*, produced by John Goldstone and directed by Terry Jones; *Greystoke*, produced and directed by Hugh Hudson; *The Boys in Blue* with top British comedy team Cannon and Ball; and the new James Bond adventure *Never Say Never Again* with Sean Connery, Barbara Carrera and Kim Basinger, produced by Jack Schwartzman and directed by Irvin Kershner.

All of these 1982 productions are already part of the studio's history as well as a dominant force for its future. Long may the industry oak planted in 1913 and cultivated by John Maxwell in 1927 continue to flourish. And long may the industry expertise that went to creat Elstree, the British Hollywood, continue to flourish with it.

The Boys in Blue, a Cannon and Ball comedy: left to right, Val Guest (director), Bobby Ball, Suzanne Danielle, Tommy Cannon and Greg Smith (producer)

Bibliography

A-Sitting on a Gate Ben Travers (W.H. Allen, 1978)

The Bioscope, 1914–1929 (Ganes)

The British Film and Television Year Books, 1946–1982 Peter Noble (Screen International Publishers)

The British Film Catalogue, 1895–1970 Denis Gifford (David and Charles, 1973)

The British Film Industry PEP Reports. Political and Economic Planning 1952, 1958

The Cinema: Its Present Position and Future Possibilities (National Council of Public Morals, 1917)

Cinema in Britain Ivan Butler (A.S. Barnes/Tantivy Press, 1973)

Close Up 1927–1933 (Pool)

Collected Screenplays of Bernard Shaw Bernard F. Dukore (George Prior, 1980)

A Critical History of British Cinema R. Armes (Secker and Warburg, 1978)

The Elstree Story (Clerke and Cockeran, 1948)

The Film Business Ernest Betts (Allen and Unwin, 1973)

Film Weekly, 1928–1929 (English Newspapers Ltd)

The Forgotten Pioneers An article by John M. East (Published in the October 1972 issue of 'Hertfordshire Countryside' by Carling and Co.)

Good Morning Boys: Will Hay Roy Seaton and Ray Martin (Barrie and Jenkins, 1978)

The Guinness Book of Film Facts and Figures Patrick Robertson (Guinness Superlatives Ltd, 1980)

Halliwell's Filmgoer's Companion, 6th edition (Granada, 1972)

Halliwell's Film Guide, 3rd edition (Granada, 1981)

History of the British Film 3 vols. R. Low (Allen and Unwin, 1949, 1971, 1973)

Hitchcock F. Truffaut (Secker and Warburg, 1968)

International Film Encyclopedia Ephraim Katz (Macmillan, 1980)

I remember Romano's Henry Kendall (Hutchinson, 1960)

Kinematograph Weekly and *Kine Weekly* 1920–1971 (Odhams Press)

Kinematograph Year Books, 1914–1970 (Odhams Press)

Launder and Gilliatt Geoff Brown (BFI, 1977)

Log of a Film Director Norman Lee (Quality Press, 1949)

Michael Balcon Presents. . . . A Lifetime of Films Michael Balcon (Hutchinson, 1969)

Miracle of the Movies Leslie Wood (Burke Publishing Co., 1947)

Nice Work Adrian Brunel, Forbes Robertson (1949)

Pictures and the Picturegoer/Picturegoer 1914–1960 (Odhams Press)

Picture Show Annual, 1926 (Odhams Press)

The Pleasure Dome Graham Greene (Secker and Warburg, 1972)

Robert Donat J.C. Trewin (Heinemann, 1968)

Screen and TV International (formerly *Cinema TV Today*) 1971 – current 1982 (King Publications Ltd)

Top Hat and Tails Michael Marshall (Elm Tree Books, 1978)

Twenty-Five Thousand Sunsets Herbert Wilcox (The Bodley Head, 1967)

Where We Came In C.A. Oakley (Allen and Unwin, 1964)

With an Independent Air Howard Thomas (Weidenfeld and Nicolson, 1977)

World Encyclopedia of Film Cawkwell and Smith (Studio Vista, 1972)

List of Films

Films produced at the B.I.P., A.B.P.C., EMI-M.G.M. and THORN-EMI Elstree Studios.

1927
Poppies of Flanders
Ring, The
Silver Lining, The
White Sheik, The

1928
Adam's Apple
Champagne
Cocktails
Farmer's Wife, The
Little Bit of Fluff, A
Manxman, The
Moulin Rouge
Not Quite a Lady
Paradise
Tommy Atkins
Toni
Week-End Wives
Widecombe Fair

1929
* Alpine Melodies
American Prisoner, The
* Arabian Knight, An
Atlantic
* Black and White
Blackmail
* Chelsea Nights
Emerald of the East
Flying Scotsman, The
Hate Ship, The
High Seas
Informer, The
* Jazztime
Kitty
Lady from the Sea, The
Lily of Killarney
* Me and the Boys
* Memories
* Musical Medley
* Musical Moments
* Notes and Notions
* Odd Numbers

* Old World Garden, An
Piccadilly
Plaything, The
* Pot-Pourri
Romance of Seville, A
* Song-Copation
Song or Two, A
Those Who Love
Under the Greenwood Tree
* Up the Poll
Vagabond Queen, The

1930
Alf's Carpet
Almost a Honeymoon
Black Hand Gang, The
Children of Chance
* Choral Cameos
* Claude Deputises
Compromising Daphne
Compulsory Husband, The
Elastic Affair, An
Elstree Calling
* Feast of Harmony, A
Flame of Love, The
* Goodbye to All That
Harmony Heaven
* Jolly Farmers, The
Juno and the Paycock
Kiss Me Sergeant
Loose Ends
Middle Watch, The
Murder
Night Birds
Not so Quiet on the Western
   Front
Raise the Roof
* Realities
Song of Soho
Suspense
* Tam O'Shanter
* Tell Tales
Two Worlds
"W" Plan, The

* We Take Off Our Hats
Why Sailors Leave Home
Young Woodley

1931
Bill and Coo
Cape Forlorn
Creeping Shadows
* Cupboard Love
Dr Josser, K.C.
Flying Fool, The
Gipsy Blood
Girl in the Night, The
Glamour
Hobson's Choice
House Opposite, The
How He Lied to Her Husband
Josser Joins the Navy
Keepers of Youth
* Lame Duck
Let's Love and Laugh
Love Habit, The
Love Lies
Love Race
Man at Six, The
Man from Morocco, The
Men Like These
Money for Nothing
My Wife's Family
O.K. Chief
Old Soldiers Never Die
Out of the Blue
Perfect Lady, The
Poor Old Bill
Potiphar's Wife
Rich and Strange
Shadow Between, The
Shadows
Skin Game, The
Strip, Strip, Hooray
Tin Gods
Tonight's the Night
Uneasy Virtue
What a Night!
Woman Between, The

1932

After Office Hours
Arms and the Man
Bachelor's Baby
Brother Alfred
* Dual Control
Fires of Fate
For the Love of Mike
His Wife's Mother
Indiscretions of Eve
Innocents of Chicago, The
Josser in the Army
Last Coupon, The
Let Me Explain Dear
Lord Camber's Ladies
Lucky Girl
Maid of the Mountains, The
Mr Bill the Conqueror
Money Talks
Number Seventeen
Old Spanish Customers
Sleepless Nights

1933

Across the Sahara
Crime on the Hill
Facing the Music
* Feather Bed, The
Happy
Hawley's of High Street
Heads We Go
I Spy
Leave It To Me
Letting in the Sunshine
Love Nest, The
My Old Duchess
On Secret Service
Pride of the Force, The
Radio Parade
Red Wagon
Scotland Yard Mystery, The
Song You Gave Me, The
Southern Maid, A
Their Night Out
Timbuctoo
You Made Me Love You

1934

Blossom Time
Doctor's Orders
Freedom of the Seas
Give Her a Ring
Girls Will Be Boys
Lost in the Legion
Luck of a Sailor, The
Master and Man
Mr Cinders
My Song Goes Round the World
Old Curiosity Shop, The

Political Party, A
Radio Parade of 1935
Those Were the Days
* Wishes

1935

Abdul the Damned
Dandy Dick
Drake of England
Heart's Desire
I Give My Heart
Invitation to the Waltz
It's A Bet
McGlusky the Sea Rover
Mimi
Music Hath Charms
Student's Romance, The

1936

Glamorous Night
Living Dangerously
Ourselves Alone
Someone at the Door
Star fell from Heaven, A
Tenth Man, The

1937

Aren't Men Beasts!
Bulldog Drummond at Bay
Dominant Sex, The
Let's Make a Night of It
Oh Boy
Please Teacher
Sensation
Spring Handicap
Terror, The

1938

Black Limelight
Hold My Hand
Housemaster
Jane Steps Out
Just Like a Woman
Luck of the Navy
Marigold
Over She Goes
Premiere
Queer Cargo
St Martin's Lane
Star of the Circus
Vessel of Wrath
Yellow Sands
Yes Madam

1939

At the Villa Rose
Black Eyes
Dead Man's Shoes

Jamaica Inn
Just William
Lucky to Me
Murder in Soho
Outsider, The
Poison Pen
She Couldn't Say No

1948

Hasty Heart, The
Man on the Run

1949

Dancing Years, The
Guilt is My Shadow
Landfall
Portrait of Clare
Stage Fright
Woman with no Name, The

1950

Captain Horatio Hornblower,
    R.N.
Elstree Story, The
Green Grow the Rushes
Happy Go Lovely
Laughter in Paradise
Young Wives' Tale

1951

Angels One Five
Castle in the Air
Magic Box, The
So Little Time
Twenty-four Hours in a
    Woman's Life
Where's Charley?
Woman's Angle, The

1952

Father's Doing Fine
Isn't Life Wonderful
Master of Ballantrae, The
South of Algiers
Top Secret
Valley of Song
Will Any Gentleman?
Yellow Balloon, The

1953

Duel in the Jungle
Good Beginning, The
Happy Ever After
House of the Arrow
Knave of Hearts
Rob Roy – the Highland Rogue
Trouble in the Glen
Weak and the Wicked, The

1954

Dam Busters, The
For Better, For Worse
Lilacs in the Spring
Moby Dick

1955

It's Great to be Young
It's Never Too Late
King's Rhapsody
Now and Forever
Oh Rosalinda!
Tarzan and the Lost Safari
Tons of Trouble
Yield to the Night
You Can't Escape

1956

Good Companions, The
Interpol
Let's Be Happy
My Wife's Family
Night of the Demon
No Time for Tears
Sea Wife, The
Silken Affair, The
Yangtse Incident

1957

Chase a Crooked Shadow
High Hell
Ice Cold in Alex
Indiscreet
Key, The
Lady Mislaid, A
Law and Disorder
Moonraker, The
Naked Earth, The
She Didn't Say No!
Silent Enemy, The
Small Hotel
These Dangerous Years
Traitors, The
Woman in a Dressing Gown
Wonderful Things
Young and the Guilty, The

1958

Alive and Kicking
Devil's Disciple, The
Flying Doctor (T.V. Series)
Girls at Sea
Intent to Kill
Lady is a Square, The
Look Back in Anger
Man Inside, The
No Trees in the Street
Operation Bullshine

Siege of Pinchgut, The
Two-Headed Spy, The

1959

Bottoms Up
Follow that Horse!
Hell is a City
Moment of Danger
School for Scoundrels
Sundowners, The
Tommy the Toreador
Two Faces of Dr Jekyll, The

1960

Don't Bother to Knock
Full Treatment, The
Hand in Hand
His and Hers
Lolita
Long and the Short and the
    Tall, The
Naked Edge, The
Rebel, The
Roman Spring of Mrs Stone,
    The
Sands of the Desert
Story of David, A
Taste of Fear, A
Trials of Oscar Wilde, The

1961

Billy Budd
Go to Blazes
Guns of Darkness
Mrs Gibbons' Boys
Night of the Eagle
Operation Snatch
Petticoat Pirates
Pot Carriers, The
Sir Francis Drake (T.V. Series)
Young Ones, The

1962

Boys, The
Dr Crippin
Jigsaw
Punch and Judy Man, The
Saint, The (T.V. Series)
Sparrows Can't Sing
Summer Holiday
We Joined the Navy

1963

Bargee, The
Cracksman, The
Crooks in Cloisters
French Dressing
Man in the Middle

Masque of the Red Death, The
Nothing but the Best
Scarlet Blade, The
Servant, The
Third Secret, The
West 11
What a Crazy World
Wonderful Life
World Ten Times Over

1964

Avengers, The (T.V. Series)
Battle at the Villa Fiorita, The
Brigand of Kandahar, The
Curse of the Mummy's Tomb
Fanatic
Gideon's Way (T.V. Series)
Human Jungle, The (T.V. Series)
Rattle of a Simple Man
She

1965

Baron, The (T.V. Series)
Double Man, The
Nanny, The
One Million Years B.C.
Slave Girls
Theatre of Death, The

1966

Avengers, The (T.V. Series 2)
Double Man, The
Mister Ten Per Cent
Saint, The (T.V. Series 3)

1967

Anniversary, The
Avengers, The (T.V. Series 3)
Champions, The (T.V. Series)
Devil Rides Out, The
Hammerhead
Lost Continent, The
Vengeance of She, The

1968

Crossplot
Department 'S' (T.V. Series)
Randall and Hopkirk (Deceased)
    (T.V. Series)
Saint, The (T.V. Series 4)
Secret Ceremony

1969

And Soon the Darkness
Crescendo
Frankenstein Must be Destroyed
Hoffman

Man Who Haunted Himself,
   The
Mr Forbush and the Penguins
Mr Jericho
Moon Zero Two
Some Will, Some Won't
Taste the Blood of Dracula

1970

Abominable Dr Phibes, The
Dulcima
Get Carter
Go-Between, The
Horror of Frankenstein, The
Lust for a Vampire
Percy
Raging Moon, The
Railway Children, The
Scars of Dracula, The
Tales of Beatrix Potter
Up Pompeii
Vampire Lovers, The

1971

Alf Garnett Saga, The
Baxter
Blood from the Mummy's Tomb
Boy Friend, The
Demons of the Mind
Dr Jekyll and Sister Hyde
Dr Phibes Rises Again
Dracula A.D. 1972
Endless Night
Fear in the Night
Henry VIII and his Six Wives
I am a Dancer (Nureyev)
Made
On the Buses
Protectors, The (T.V. series)
Rentadick
Up the Chastity Belt
Villain

1972

Adolf Hitler – My Part in his
   Downfall
Best Pair of Legs in the
   Business, The
Captain Kronos
* Cobblers of Umbridge, The
Digby, the Biggest Dog in the
   World
Doll's House, A
Father Dear Father
Final Programme, The
For the Love of Ada
Frankenstein and the Monster
   from Hell
Legend of Hell House, The

Little Prince, The
Mutiny on the Buses
National Health, The
Neither the Sea nor the Sand
Night Watch
Not Now Darling
Our Miss Fred
Protectors, The (T.V. Series 2)
Satanic Rites of Dracula, The
Straight On Till Morning
Up the Front

1973

Holiday on the Buses
Love Thy Neighbour
Man at the Top
Swallows and Amazons
Take Me High
Vampira

1974

Alfie Darling
Confessions of a Window
   Cleaner
Galileo
Great Expectations
In Celebration
Maids, The
Man about the House
Murder on the Orient Express
Out of Season
Percy's Progress
To the Devil a Daughter

1975

Confessions of a Pop Performer
Hedda
Keep It Up Downstairs
Likely Lads, The
Spanish Fly
Voyage of the Damned

1976

Confessions of a Driving
   Instructor
Julia
Not Now Comrade
Stand Up Virgin Soldiers
Star Wars
Valentino

1977

Are You Being Served?
Confessions from a Holiday
   Camp
Greek Tycoon, The
Hanover Street
Return of the Saint, The (T.V.
   Series)

Rosie Dixon Night Nurse
Shining, The
Spectre
Suspense

1978

Amahl and the Night Visitors
Empire Strikes Back, The
Man Called Intrepid, A
Murder by Decree
Stevie

1979

Flash Gordon (part)
Never Never Land

1980

Final Conflict, The
George and Mildred
Great Muppet Caper, The
Green Ice
Monster Club, The
Raiders of the Lost Ark
Shillingbury Tales (part)
Venom

1981

Dark Crystal
Death in Venice
Lady Chatterley's Lover
Oliver Twist (T.V. Production)
Return of the Jedi

1982

Greystoke: The Creation of
   Tarzan And His Epic
   Adventures
Monty Python's Meaning of Life
Never Say Never Again
Reilly

N.B. Films indicated by an * are
shorts
The very nature of Elstree: the
British Hollywood meant that
some productions overflowed
into other Elstree studios and in
some cases the B.I.P. films were
either started or finished at the
B.I.P. Welwyn studios. Added to
which, many independent
producers and their
productions, would move from
one Elstree studio to another.
This film list was compiled from
the B.I.P., A.B.P.C., EMI-M.G.M.
and THORN-EMI 'Made at
Elstree' lists and records.

Index